CULTURE SMART!

BRAZIL

THE ESSENTIAL GUIDE TO CUSTOMS & CULTURE

SANDRA BRANCO

KUPERARD

"The real voyage of discovery consists not in seeking new landscapes, but in having new eyes."

Adapted from Marcel Proust, *Remembrance of Things Past*.

ISBN 978 1 78702 339 0

British Library Cataloguing in Publication Data
A CIP catalogue entry for this book is available
from the British Library

First published in Great Britain
by Kuperard, an imprint of Bravo Ltd
59 Hutton Grove, London N12 8DS
Tel: +44 (0) 20 8446 2440
www.culturesmart.co.uk
Inquiries: publicity@kuperard.co.uk

Design Bobby Birchall
Printed in Türkiye by Elma Basim

The Culture Smart! series is continuing to expand.
All Culture Smart! guides are available as e-books, and many
as audio books. For further information and latest titles visit
www.culturesmart.co.uk

ABOUT THE AUTHOR

SANDRA BRANCO is a Brazilian-born writer now living in the UK. After graduating in Communications from São Paulo University she worked as a TV producer and scriptwriter in São Paulo, Rio de Janeiro, Recife, Bahia, and Ceará, and gained national prizes for her work in educational television. She went on to obtain an MA in Screenwriting at the Northern School of Film and Television in Leeds. In the UK, Sandra has worked for the Brazilian Embassy and the University of Westminster, contributing to the MA program in International Liaison and Communication. She has traveled widely and takes a keen interest in art and film worldwide. Today Sandra lives and works in London and visits Brazil regularly.

CONTENTS

"Brazil is not for amateurs"

Tom Jobim, bossa nova legend

For many, Brazil conjures up images of Carnaval, the Amazon rainforest, football, and the finest coffee in the world. But there is much more to this country than beaches and bossa nova, though the sound of samba might be an excellent starting point for exploring this vibrant and complex land.

Brazil is at once stunningly beautiful and delightfully disorganized. It is one of the ten largest economies in the world, yet poverty exists side by side with spectacular wealth. As part of the New World, it is open to new ideas, new technologies, and newcomers, and yet conservative values are deeply held by many. Youthful and fast-moving, the country can overwhelm you with its sheer size, or the warmth and spontaneity of its people, while its street children and shantytowns can be quite unsettling.

The fundamental thing to understand is that there is not one Brazil but several, not only because of its varied geography, regional differences, and ethnic mix, but also in time: centuries-old habits coexist alongside modern lifestyles. It is also a true melting pot of cultures and population that you will better get to know throughout these pages. And yet despite all of this, there is a strong sense of national identity.

To put things into context, Brazil is the biggest country in South America and the fifth largest in the world. It builds satellites, exports airplanes, has its own petroleum industry, and takes pride in its modern architecture, furniture, fashion, and picturesque colonial towns. It has four different time zones, a rainforest, an Atlantic forest, drylands, wetlands, flatlands, high mountains, skyscrapers, busy urban centers, and quite a few deserted beaches hidden away along its 4,655 mile (7,491 km) coastline.

One cannot hope to do justice to such diversity in a single book, so some generalization is inevitable. *Culture Smart! Brazil* aims to help you discover this fascinating country for yourself. In the chapters that follow you will be introduced to the Brazilian people, their values, customs, and traditions; how they go about their daily life, socialize, and spend their leisure time; and the way they think and do business. You will become familiar with the historical circumstances and influences that have shaped Brazilian society, and perhaps most importantly, will be given the tools to communicate effectively across the cultural divide and so, should you hope to, build relationships with those you'll meet along the way.

Official Name	Republica Federativa do Brasil (Federal Republic of Brazil)	
Population	217 million	
Capital City	Brasília	Pop. 4.9 milllion
Major Cities (by Population)	São Paulo, Rio de Janeiro, Belo Horizonte, Porto Alegre, Brasília, Recife, Salvador, Curitiba	
Area	3,286,470 sq. miles (8,511,965 sq. km)	
Climate	Tropical and subtropical	
Currency	Real	1 real = 100 centavos
Ethnic Makeup	White 47.7%; Mixed Race 43.1%; Black 7.6%; Oriental 1.1%; Indigenous 0.4%	
Language	Portuguese	
Main Religions	No official religion. Predominantly Roman Catholic. Growing Evangelical movement	Other religions include: Mormons, Eastern Orthodox, Judaism, Islam, Buddhism, and Spiritualism (Kardecism, African, and Native Indian).
Government	Federal Republic, governed by Executive, Legislature, and Judiciary at national and state levels	Bicameral legislature: the Chamber of Deputies and the Senate. Presidential elections are held every four years.

Economy	Average annual GDP growth of 0.6% over last decade.	Main trade partners are China, USA, Argentina, Germany, Netherlands, and Chile.
Media	The main network TV channels are Globo, SBT, Record, and Bandeirantes. Main paid TV providers are NET, SKY, Claro TV, VIVO TV, Oi TV, and GVT TV. There are over 9,000 radio stations.	The newspapers with the widest circulation are *O Globo*, *Folha de São Paulo*, *O Estado de São Paulo*, *Valor Econômico*, and *Jornal do Brasil*.
English Language Media	*Folha International*, *The Brazilian Report*, *The Rio Times*, *Valor Econômico*	
Electricity	220 volts and/or 110–127 volts	Several electricity grids supply electricity at different voltages.
Internet Domain	.br	
Telephone	Country code: +55	The code for dialing out depends on the phone company you use.
Time Zone	There are four time zones: Standard Brasília Time, GMT minus 3 hours (majority of the country); Western Area, GMT minus 4 hours; Acre, GMT minus 5 hours; Fernando de Noronha, GMT minus 2 hours.	Some parts of the country adopt summer time (generally from October to February).

CHAPTER ONE

LAND & PEOPLE

If you could choose only one word to describe Brazil, it should probably be "diverse." The variety of landscape, climate, flora, fauna, ethnicities, belief systems, and lifestyles is enormous by any standard.

Brazilians tend to think of their country as some sort of continent within South America, likely because its land mass represents nearly half the entire territory (47.3 percent, to be exact). Looking at a map, we can see that to the east of Brazil lies the Atlantic Ocean, which forms 4,600 miles (7,400 km) of sun-kissed coastline that includes more than two thousand beaches, while the west side borders all other South American countries, bar Chile and Ecuador.

Since Brazil is mostly situated south of the equator, the seasons are the reverse of those in Europe and the USA. Officially, summer lasts from December 22 to March 21, fall from March 22 to June 21, winter from June 22 to September 21, and spring from September 22 to December 21. In parts of the country, however, notably the Amazon region, seasonal divisions are less clearly marked and tend to be classified as "wet" and "dry."

Brazil has four time zones. Brasília time is the nation's official standard, three hours behind Greenwich Mean Time (GMT), London.

The equator crosses the north of the country, near the city of Macapá. The Tropic of Capricorn passes through the south, near the city of São Paulo. This means that most of the country is within the tropical zone and characterized by a hot and humid climate. However, tropical does not necessarily mean that every region is hot all year round, nor that the countryside is filled with lush vegetation. Altitude, proximity to the sea, soil fertility, and prevailing winds and weather fronts all have an effect on the different regions of the country.

Generally speaking, the north is hotter and the south cooler (temperatures in some parts can fall below zero and snow is even seen occasionally in some cities). Cities on the coast are more humid, while those located on plateaus inland, such as Brasília, São Paulo, and Belo Horizonte, have more temperate climates, though climate change has led to an overall rise in average temperatures.

More specifically, Brazil can be divided into six climate zones: equatorial, tropical, Atlantic tropical, semiarid, highland tropical, and subtropical, according to location and terrain.

BRAZIL'S CLIMATE ZONES

In the Amazon region, which is equatorial, temperatures average 71–79°F (22–26°C), though at times it can be much hotter, and it rains often and heavily. Indeed, there are two areas where rainfall reaches over 78 inches (2,000 mm) a year: in the upper Amazon and near the city of Belém.

Most of central Brazil, parts of the northeast, and parts of the southeast have a tropical climate, characterized by hot, humid summers and colder, drier winters. Average temperature is around 68°F (20°C).

As its name suggests, the Atlantic tropical climate zone affects the coastline from Rio Grande do Norte down to the state of Paraná. Here rainfall is intense at different times of the year (fall and winter in the northeast and summer in the south). Temperatures can vary between 64 and 79°F (18 and 26°C), though as with other parts of the country they can rise to near 100°F (38°C) in summer.

The dryland inland part of the northeast, or *sertão*, is semiarid and suffers from long periods of drought. Temperatures average 80°F (27°C) but can soar above 100°F (38°C).

Along the plateau that stretches across the

southeastern states of São Paulo, Minas Gerais, and parts of Paraná and Mato Grosso do Sul (highland tropical), temperatures average around 64–71°F (18–22°C). Rainfall can be very heavy during the summer. In the area along the border of the mountain range (Serra do Mar) in the state of São Paulo it rains almost as much as in the Amazon. However, winters are drier with occasional frost in some areas.

The area south of the Tropic of Capricorn has a subtropical climate. Here, despite hot summers, average temperatures are lower than 64°F (18°C) and can drop below freezing in winter.

THE REGIONS

Brazil is divided into five administrative regions. The characteristics of their inhabitants are highly influenced by their geographic and economic situations.

North
Amazonas – Pará – Acre – Rondônia – Roraima – Amapá – Tocantins

Also known as the Amazon region, the North region is home to over half of the planet's remaining rainforest. Sparsely populated, most of the region's inhabitants

The mighty Amazon River.

are concentrated in urban areas. It rains often and so regularly that locals tend to organize their day by it, dividing errands and appointments to "before the rain" and "after the rain."

The Amazon River is the world's largest in volume and its annual outflow accounts for one fifth of the world's fresh water entering the sea. It is not surprising, then, that much of the transport in the region is by boat.

The region has powerful folklore traditions, largely of Indigenous origin, that are kept alive by the *caboclos*—the mixed descendants of Portuguese and Indigenous peoples.

Reservations have been set up for the different

Indigenous groups that live in the region. Most of these groups maintain contact with Brazilian institutions, though for a variety of reasons, a few do not welcome strangers. It is thought that there are still more Indigenous groups living in the Amazon that have yet to come into contact with outsiders.

Given the difficulty policing such a vast and uninhabited natural area, illegal settlers, loggers, traders, and drug traffickers have taken advantage of the situation. There have sometimes also been violent clashes with the Indigenous groups and the continued illegal activity threatens their survival.

The harvesting of Brazil nuts and rubber latex are still the region's main economic activities, in addition to logging, mining, farming, and manufacturing. Ecotourism in the area has grown in recent years, but plays only a small role comparatively.

For many years, agriculture and mining in the region were encouraged. This led to jungle-sized environmental problems and the deforestation of about 19 percent of the entire rainforest (an area larger than France). Deforestation peaked in 2004, but a series of government policies implemented by the government of Luiz Inácio Lula da Silva ("Lula"), such as the prohibition of timber export, slowed deforestation by 84 percent by 2013. The rate of deforestation decreased during the decade that followed, but for many in the region and the wider world fears over the long-term environmental impacts of the loss of rainforest habitat remain. According to environmental scientists, the Amazon forest plays a critical role in stabilizing the global climate: around 123 billion tons of carbon is stored in the Amazon rainforest, while its trees release 22 billion tons of water into the atmosphere per day, playing a critical role in global carbon and water cycles. As a result of deforestation, the Amazon is becoming hotter, drier, and more prone to wildfires and, if the trend is to continue, part of the rainforest may become savanna, and this would have far-reaching ramifications for regional and global climates. A zero-deforestation commitment announced at the outset of Lula's 2022 reelection hopes to reverse the destructive process.

In terms of wildlife habitat, the Amazon rainforest is the largest single reserve of biological organisms in the world. Even though nobody knows how many different species inhabit it, scientists estimate that they represent 15–30 percent of all species on the planet.

The two main cities in the North are Manaus and Belém do Pará, which have a population of 2.2 million and 1.4 million respectively.

The state of Acre and the western corner of the state of Amazonas are five hours behind GMT and two hours behind Brasília Time, while the rest of Amazonas, and the states of Rondônia, Roraima, and the western half of the state of Pará are four hours behind GMT or one hour behind Brasília Time. The eastern half of Pará and the state of Tocantins are three hours behind GMT at standard Brasília Time.

Salvador city in the Northeastern state of Bahia.

Northeast
*Maranhão – Piauí – Ceará – Rio Grande do Norte –
Paraíba – Pernambuco – Bahia – Alagoas – Sergipe –
Fernando de Noronha (island territory)*

Perhaps the biggest contrasts within any region can
be found in the Northeast. The region is the second
most populous in Brazil, and the difference in lifestyle
between its rich and poor inhabitants is marked.

The region's Atlantic coastline is beautiful, and
its palm beaches and warm waters attract both
considerable domestic and foreign tourism. The land
on the coastal plain is very fertile and devoted mainly
to sugar plantations. In the interior, however, lie the

drylands, or *sertão*. This area suffers regular and lengthy droughts, resulting in large-scale misery and migration. The people of this area (*sertanejos*) leave their homes either to work in the sugar plantations during the drought period, or for good, opting instead for urban centers in the Northeast and Southeast regions. Once there many can struggle to secure regular employment, however, and must persevere through challenging circumstances.

The transitional zone between the coastal plain and the *sertão* is called the *agreste* and is devoted to cattle rearing. In the cities the service sector plays an important economic role. Since the discovery of sizable oil fields off the coastline, the region has attracted greater domestic and international investment.

The states of Pernambuco and Bahia, where most of the oil fields were found, were key colonial centers and their resonance in Brazilian culture is strong. They have a very rich folklore tradition that has inspired most of the music, cuisine, and much of the culture that is today considered to be "typically Brazilian."

The region was also home to numerous resistance centers, or *quilombos*. These were self-sufficient communities created by black slaves who had managed to escape the difficult conditions of colonial-era plantations. The most successful of these were in Pernambuco. Today, Salvador, capital of Bahia, is the center for black culture and consciousness in Brazil.

Among the region's inhabitants, those who live on

the coast tend to be more laid-back than those inland. Indeed, they say the *sertanejos* are as tough as the land they live on. Because of the heat, whenever possible, Northeasterners have longer lunch hours and will sometimes take a half-hour nap after lunch. However, services and shops do not tend to close for lunch and work normal commercial hours.

The development of tourism and preserving the environment are key concerns in this region, and this was not helped by an oil spill in 2019. Around 1,400 miles (2,250 kms) of coastline were affected and an estimated 4,000 tons of crude oil washed up onto beaches in the following months. Local communities led the clean-up with support from the army. Despite the damage caused to natural habitats, fishing communities on the coast, and the local tourism industry, the region's economy is bouncing back. In 2022, the government invested heavily in infrastructure, including modernizing airports, asphalting roads, and the development of waterfront areas; 268 such projects received funding. In 2023 all seven major cities in the region featured among Brazil's top 20 cities for business investment.

The largest cities in the Northeast are Salvador and Fortaleza, with population sizes of 2.9 million and 2.7 million people respectively.

The entire Northeast region is three hours behind GMT at standard Brasília Time, except for Fernando de Noronha, which is two hours behind GMT and one hour ahead of standard Brasília Time.

The Oscar Nieyemer-designed National Congress Palace in Brasília.

Central West
Mato Grosso – Mato Grosso do Sul – Goiás – Federal District of Brasília

This region covers most of the country's central plateau (*planalto central*). An area of widespread savannas and tropical grasslands, it is still sparsely populated.

In order to encourage migration and development in the remote and isolated Central West region, President Kubitschek (1955–60) moved Brazil's capital from Rio de Janeiro to "the middle of nowhere," as some called it then. The result was the planned city of Brasília, the "capital of hope." For many years, however, Brasília remained a dormitory city for politicians. It can still feel a little bit like an overgrown university campus, where you need to drive or take the bus to go across town and where sidewalks do not exist on the main roads. The place is nonetheless lightened by the stunning curves of buildings by architect Oscar Niemeyer.

The region is also home to one of Brazil's most famous ecotourist destinations, the Pantanal swamplands in Mato Grosso. People come to explore diverse fauna and flora, see multitudes of colorful birds, and spot caimans.

Due to a rapid expansion in industrial farming, the savanna ecosystem has suffered a great deal, being reduced to less than 20 percent of its original size. Agro-industry and cattle-raising remain the major economic activities.

The federal government has demarcated areas in the region as reservations for the Indigenous groups who lived there prior to colonial settlement. Although the majority of Brazilians express protective views about these groups and their right to the land, those who live near the reservations have more mixed opinions. Some people seem to resent the fact that the tribes are given a lot of land while they have to work hard to buy a small plot.

In spite of state efforts and a slow increase in migration to the area, some parts of the region remain remote, allowing for exploitative work practices to take place.

The main cities in the Central West are Brasília (pop. 4.9 million), Goiânia (pop. 1.6 million), and Campo Grande (pop. 950,000).

Mato Grosso and Mato Grosso do Sul are four hours behind GMT and one hour behind Brasília Time. The Federal District of Brasília and the state of Goiás are three hours behind GMT at standard Brasília Time.

Southeast
*Minas Gerais – Espírito Santo – Rio de Janeiro –
São Paulo*

Most of Brazil's population is concentrated in this
region. It has been called "the heart of Brazil" (or
sometimes its "brain") because of the major economic
role it plays. Here, both industry and agriculture are
the most developed of any region, while the city of
São Paulo is both the main financial and commercial
center of the country.

Downtown São Paulo.

The Southeast is rich in minerals and gems; it produces coffee and grains for export, plus a variety of foodstuffs, dairy, and meat products for the domestic market. It is also the traditional manufacturing base of the country. Tourism plays a significant part in the region's economy, particularly in the city of Rio de Janeiro and the historic towns of Minas Gerais. Minas contains a series of well-kept picturesque colonial towns with some of the best examples of Brazilian baroque art, which is unique and less ornate than the European version.

The coastline is stunningly framed by the mountains of the Serra do Mar, with some preserved areas of Atlantic forest. Mountain formations are everywhere and characterize some of the famous images of Brazil, such as the Pão de Açúcar (Sugar Loaf Mountain) in Rio.

São Paulo state is a land of immigrants, with descendants from all groups who declare themselves proud Brazilians and *paulistas* (inhabitants of São Paulo state). Its capital, also called São Paulo, is the largest metropolitan area in the country and ranks fourth in the world, with a population of over 22 million. It is a popular destination for tourists and especially so for business travelers. *Paulistanos*, the inhabitants of São Paulo city, are individualistic, dynamic, and are known for their work ethic. Most work long hours and many have more than one job. It is truly a cosmopolitan center and the international influence of its inhabitants is reflected in the city's cuisine and art. Today, there are more Italians and Italian descendants in São Paulo than in Rome, while in the district of Liberdade there is a Japanese community that has been resident in the city since 1912 and which keeps pre-war Japanese customs and traditions!

Being such a large and populous city, personal safety is also a concern, which explains why eight hundred bullet proof vehicles are sold here every month. The wealthy have also taken to using helicopters to get around, though this is in part to avoid the city's dire traffic jams. As a result, São Paulo has the largest fleet of helicopters in the world—more than New York or Tokyo.

Ouro Preto city in Minas Gerais.

Rio de Janeiro remains the Brazilian picture postcard for foreigners and the main tourist destination, especially during Carnaval. Brazil's second-largest city, Rio de Janeiro has a population of some 7 million people and is renowned for its laid-back charm and beach lifestyle, epitomised by Disney Studios 1940s samba-loving character "Zé Carioca." It is home to the mega studios of TV Globo, the most influential national network and one of the largest in the world (see The Media, Chapter 9). *Cariocas* (inhabitants of Rio) claim theirs is Brazil's most beautiful city and contest São Paulo's claim to being the most important.

As you might have guessed, there is a permanent rivalry between Rio and São Paulo that although sometimes disguised, can be found in the most unsuspecting places and so visitors socializing or doing business in either city should be cautious before expressing a strong opinion about one or the other. Despite their claims, residents of both Rio de Janeiro and São Paulo share the harsh realities of pollution, traffic, noise, violence, and crime.

Mineiros, people from Minas Gerais, are thought of as serious and hardworking. They can be more private and reserved on initial contact compared to other Brazilians, but they are very hospitable.

The state capitals in the Southeast are Belo Horizonte, Vitória, Rio de Janeiro, and São Paulo.

The entire Southeast region is three hours behind GMT at standard Brasília Time.

South

Paraná – Santa Catarina – Rio Grande do Sul

With a cooler climate, the South is considered to offer the best quality of life and is a highly developed region, with major cattle-raising and agricultural industries, including grain production and wine making. It is also home to Itaipú, one of the largest hydroelectric dams in the world.

The coast of Santa Catarina, in particular the city of Florianópolis, is a popular summer tourist destination for domestic visitors as well as considerable numbers of Argentinians.

Located on the border between Brazil, Argentina, and Paraguay is one of Brazil's most prominent nature reserves, the Iguaçu National Park. Home to the Iguaçu Falls that is made up of three hundred stunning waterfalls, it is a UNESCO World Heritage Site and provides habitat for sixteen hundred animal species, a number of which are endangered, such as the purple-winged ground dove. It is also the last jaguar refuge in southern Brazil. A 2021 plan to revive a road that cuts through the park has been met with heavy opposition from local and international environmental groups who warned that it will encourage illegal poaching and logging in the biodiversity hotspot in addition to the loss of habitat the construction will cause. Congress passed a bill in 2021 that called for the reopening of the road but as of 2023, it remains closed.

Iguaçu Falls includes more than three hundred waterfalls and is a UNESCO World Heritage Site.

In the past, the southern highlands were covered in subtropical forest with a predominance of *araucária* pine trees. However, the expansion of agro-industry resulted in heavy deforestation of the area and just a few pockets of pine forest remain.

Further south, the wide plains of the Pampas are shared with Uruguay and Argentina. Heartland of the *gaúchos*, South American cowboys, the Pampas is where they once hunted wild cattle and drank *chimarrão*, a strong tea made of the herb *maté*, prepared and served in a bowl with a silver straw. Drinking the caffeine-rich *chimarrão* is one of the best-kept traditions of this region. The term *gaúcho* was originally used to describe the mixed descendants of Portuguese, Spanish, and Indigenous Guarani populations. Nowadays it refers to all Rio Grande do Sul inhabitants. Porto Alegre, the capital of Rio Grande do Sul, is the state's commercial center and a hub for leather tanning and shipbuilding industries. The discovery of offshore oil reserves in recent years has also boosted the city's port and economic activity.

The region cherishes its European heritage, being substantially composed of German, Italian, Slav, and Polish immigrant descendants. Blumenau, in Santa Catarina, is the center of German culture in Brazil, following the Germanic festive calendar and keeping its traditions and cuisine, with an architecture to match. Meanwhile, the Italian immigrants of Rio Grande do Sul are recognized for cultivating the country's first vineyards.

Curitiba, the capital of Paraná, has attracted much internal migration over the years. The once model city's public transportation system inspired metropolises around the world, though more recently the city's reputation has been tarnished by increasing social issues. Contemporary projects in sustainable urban planning and clean vehicle technology have seen Curitiba regain some of its status.

The main cities in the South are Florianópolis, Blumenau, Curitiba, and Porto Alegre.

The entire South is three hours behind GMT at standard Brasília Time.

POPULATION

Brazil's population is now estimated at over 215 million, ranking it firmly in the ten most populous countries in the world and the second most populous in the Americas. Much of the country is sparsely populated, however, and so the overall population density is low. Most people congregate in the cities on the coast and in the Southeast, which, as we've seen, is the center of the nation's industrial activity. Close to 50 percent of Brazil's population reside in the state of São Paulo alone.

Brazil is no longer a "young" country—in 2023 the average age of the population was thirty-three. Life expectancy is slowly rising, and population growth is now in decline, a combination of trends that spells problems for the country's economic forecast, as it does for many countries around the world. Compounding matters, Brazil has one of the lowest fertility rates in Latin America, reported to be as low as 1.7 children per woman in 2023, which is akin to that of the USA and much of Europe. To what extent this trajectory can be mitigated by technological advances remains to be seen.

Ethnicity and Race

Brazil is a truly multiethnic society. Approximately 50 percent of the population identify as "mixed race," while some 40 percent identify as "white," and about 9 percent as "black." The remainder is divided between Indigenous ethnic groups (of which there are more than three hundred!) and Asians, such as the descendants of Japanese migrants.

Of those who belong to Brazil's Indigenous ethnic groups, about 60 percent live in protected territories and many maintain a lifestyle that predates the arrival of the Europeans. Today, Indigenous territories cover approximately 10 percent of Brazil's total landmass, which, to put things in perspective, is roughly equivalent to three times the size of Great Britain.

When you compare racial background and distribution of wealth, the image is not a positive one. Historically, when slavery was abolished, black labor was replaced by immigrant labor, and black communities struggled to find their place in society or to develop strong economic networks. A lot has changed since then, but probably not enough. Nowadays there are examples of very wealthy black Brazilians in the business world, but the majority of Afro-Brazilians are found in the less wealthy classes. In order to address the situation, a system of quotas has been implemented, guaranteeing them, for example, a percentage of places in universities, similar to the system used in the USA. The scheme has been somewhat successful, though implementing it has not been simple. In a highly mixed society, deciding who is "black" is not a straightforward matter.

So, What Is a Brazilian?

As we've seen, Brazil's population is made up of

Indigenous peoples, descendants of black African slaves, and descendants of white European settlers, while the majority are a mix thereof. As such, society has developed specific terms for each combination of backgrounds. For example, the term *mulatos* refers to those who are of mixed white European and black African heritage, while *caboclos* describes those who are of mixed Indigenous and European heritage. *Mamelucos* refers to those who are of mixed Indigenous and African heritage. Today, most Brazilians of mixed heritage refer to themselves colloquially as *moreno* (lit. dark).

Apart from Portuguese, Spanish, and Dutch arrivals during colonial times, and later Italian, German, and Polish immigration, other large groups include immigrants from the Middle East, particularly Syria and Lebanon, and Japan.

More recently arrived communities include Koreans and South American nationals from neighboring countries.

As a rule, the Brazilian "love for the mixture" seems to be contagious and most groups end up contributing to the birth of new generations of colorful nationals. There is a nationwide feeling that every newcomer will enrich the original culture with their new set of practices and beliefs. One Brazilian pastime (and a way to start a conversation) is to ask someone for their surname, trying to guess their origins. Although Brazilians might come in all shapes, colors, and sizes, acceptance of difference is one thing that defines their identity.

Just How Mixed Are Brazilians?

"The Mormons in the United States had this rule that if you were black, you couldn't be a bishop in the church. When they came to Brazil, they couldn't decide who was black and so they changed the rule."

Historian Peter Burke

A BRIEF HISTORY

From the Jungle

Evidence of Paleo-Indians in the territory that later became Brazil goes back at least ten thousand years. By analyzing remains such as ceramic and cave art, archeologists have found that some Indigenous groups achieved a high level of cultural development.

There were a multitude of tribes scattered throughout the land with different customs and over one hundred and seventy languages. Along the coast, the largest ones, or those that survived colonization, were the Tupis and the Guaranis, and most of the information about Indigenous

An eleventh-century funeral urn belonging to the Indigenous Marajoara culture.

An illustration of a Tupi woman by Dutch artist Albert Eckhout.

habits and beliefs refers to the Tupi-Guarani group.

Before the Europeans arrived, Indigenous people lived mainly in seminomadic tribal communities. The extended family shared the same habitation (*oca*), which was effectively a large communal hut where each member had the use of a hammock. Cooking was done outside by the women, who took turns in doing the domestic work, including taking care of all children from the community, not only their own. The men were responsible for tasks such as hunting and fishing, besides protecting their tribe. Each tribe had a chief (*cacique*) and a witch doctor (*pajé*), both male. The *pajé* was also in charge of the religious ceremonies, which were mostly for the men only. They were polytheists and their gods were mainly connected to nature, and arranged in a hierarchy, with the principal deity being Tupã, the Thunder God. Each tribe was autonomous, with no superior governing power.

Discovery

In spite of indications of a previous European presence, Brazil was officially "discovered" by the Portuguese navigator Pedro Álvares Cabral in April 1500. Cabral was apparently on an expedition to find the western route to India when a storm blew him off course, forcing him to land in a quiet bay in today's state of Bahia.

First reports equated the lush vegetation and the innocence of the new land's naked inhabitants with visions of an earthly paradise. This comparison did not survive closer inspection, with evidence of cannibalism among some of the tribes. Failing to identify easy riches such as gold and precious stones, the colonizers settled for exploiting a lucrative red

A depiction of Cabral spotting land that would later become known as Brazil, by Brazilian painter Aurélio de Figueiredo (1854-1916).

dyewood known as *pau brasil* ("brazilwood"), which later gave its name to the country. Portuguese and French traders soon started shipping the timber to Europe.

Agriculture was the next step forward, but that was easier said than done since it meant living side by side with the Indigenous peoples. There was no central power to overthrow, and the settlers could not survive without the locals' knowledge of the forest. The only way to occupy the land was by reaching an agreement with the Indigenous groups that allowed the colonizers to share part of that knowledge. Such a pact could certainly not be achieved by force. The settlers stumbled across the solution in the strangest of circumstances.

According to the Indigenous tradition the only way to accept a stranger into a tribe was by blood ties, as the first Europeans to marry Indigenous women according to local custom found out. These were adventurous individuals who came looking for quick wealth and ended up staying, living with the tribes and taking advantage of the power that came with being both Indian and European.

Indigenous people had no concept of sin, but the Catholic Portuguese did. Although the first men to accept Indigenous values and live in accordance with them were fundamental to the colonization project, they were despised by their Christian colleagues. Once more, local customs came to the rescue. The traditional way of forming an alliance with a neighboring tribe was by offering a woman in marriage to its chief. The woman would then accept the customs of her husband's tribe instead of her own. With the proliferation of European communities and the arrival of Catholic priests, this arrangement enabled the new marriages to be accepted by both cultures. The new bride was declared "white" in the Portuguese community and the groom was considered "Indian" in his wife's tribe. This phenomenon formed the basis of a positive attitude with regard to racial mixing. But the Portuguese government used it as a form of control. It issued "purity of blood" certificates in exchange for "good behavior" and obedience from the new generations of mixed-race Brazilians, and this underlined the importance of being "white."

Colonial Government

São Vicente, in today's coastal state of São Paulo, was the first Portuguese-organized settlement, founded in 1532. Salvador was established in 1549 by Brazil's first royal governor. More needed to be done, however, in order to encourage commercial exploration and development. The Portuguese government divided the colony into fifteen areas of land (some bigger than Portugal) and made them "hereditary captaincies." These were given as a present from the king, and their owners (*donatários*) were supposed to maintain, defend, and exploit their land. This created a system of large estates that would influence the country throughout its history until modern times.

The captaincy of Pernambuco was very profitable as a result of highly productive sugar plantations. In order to work the land, the colonizers tried to enslave the Indigenous peoples, but their work rate and productivity were low. They also had no immunity to Western diseases and many died. The solution was to import slave labor from West Africa. The sugar they produced was then exported to an eager European market.

No More Boundaries

Portugal and Spain had an agreement (the Treaty of Tordesillas, 1494) that divided any land discovered in the western hemisphere between the two countries. This line crossed the middle of modern Brazilian territory. With the death of the Portuguese King Dom Sebastião in 1578, his cousin the Spanish king united both nations under the Spanish crown. As there were no boundaries, the Brazilians went on inland expeditions searching for Eldorado and capitalized on anything they found, such as precious stones and slaves. When Portugal recovered its independence from Spain in 1640, they kept the occupied lands. The Portuguese also succeeded in recovering the city of Olinda (Pernambuco) from a twenty-four-year Dutch occupation.

The First Synagogue of the Americas

When the Portuguese overthrew the Dutch, they also banished the Jews who had settled in Pernambuco. They were well established and in 1634 had already founded the first synagogue of the Americas in today's city of Recife. Once expelled, twenty-three of the Jews went to New Amsterdam (now New York) and founded the first Jewish community in what would become the USA.

The Golden Years

With the decline of Brazil's sugar economy, more inland expeditions were organized to search for gold and precious stones. Gold and diamonds were found in today's state of Minas Gerais (which means "general mines"). As a result, in 1763 the capital was moved south from Salvador to Rio de Janeiro, which was closer and a more direct link to Minas. The gold rush attracted both people from the northeastern coastal plantations and newcomers from Portugal. Much of Brazil's gold ended up in Britain through the purchase of textile products by the Portuguese and, according to some, helped pay for the British Industrial Revolution.

Just when the mining boom was weakening, an even greater source of riches materialized in the shape of coffee plantations further south.

The Kingdom of Portugal, the Algarve, and Brazil
In 1808, the Portuguese monarch and his court
transferred from Lisbon to Rio de Janeiro to escape
Napoleon's invasion of Portugal. This cunning plan
resulted in Brazil being promoted in 1815 from
colony to kingdom (as part of the Kingdom of
Portugal, the Algarve, and Brazil) and, paradoxically,
created favorable circumstances for Brazil's future
independence.

Independence Days
Although Napoleon's reign ended in 1815, the
Portuguese King João VI chose to stay in Brazil until
1821, when a political crisis threatened his power back

home. He returned to
Lisbon but left behind
his son, Pedro, with the
title of Viceroy Regent.
Barely a year after his
father's departure, the
prince proclaimed Brazil's
independence and had
himself crowned Emperor
Pedro I, even though
he remained heir to the
Portuguese throne. In
order to be recognized as
independent by Portugal,
the new Brazilian

Portrait of Emperor Pedro I by painter Simplício
Rodrigues de Sá (1785-1839).

government agreed to take over the very large debt the Portuguese owed Britain.

Emperor Dom Pedro abdicated the throne of Brazil in 1831, in favor of his son, Dom Pedro II, and returned to Lisbon to become King Pedro IV of Portugal.

Brazilian Monarchy

Dom Pedro II ruled for more than half a century. He was a competent administrator who advanced Brazil's political development and unity. His stable reign saw improvements to the infrastructure, the building of railroads, encouragement of immigration from Europe, and the consideration of health and welfare schemes for the whole country. Another change to the economy was the increase in coffee production, overtaking sugar as the national crop and accounting for well over half of the country's total exports.

Support for the monarchy came mainly from the wealthy owners of coffee plantations, which depended on slave labor. The abolition

Emperor Pedro II, 1885.

43

of slavery in 1888, in response to British pressure,
set off a reaction among the Emperor's supporters,
generating a series of parliamentary crises. In
November 1889, Dom Pedro was deposed by the
military, to the surprise of the general public. The
transition to a republic happened without bloodshed
as the royal family left the country for exile in
France.

A Land of Immigrants

Leaving aside the European colonizers, the first wave
of immigration, although not voluntary, occurred
when millions of Africans were imported to work
as slaves in the Brazilian plantations (from 1534
to 1888). The second wave was in 1808, when the
country opened its ports to "friendly nations." Both
emperors promoted European immigration, mainly
to Brazil's south. Germans and Italians were offered
plots of land and settled initially in today's states of
Santa Catarina and Rio Grande do Sul.

The most significant influx, however, took place
with the abolition of slavery. A change of policy
meant that the new immigrants would no longer be
small farmers but would come to work in the coffee
plantations as laborers. Italians, Spaniards, and, later,
Japanese established themselves mostly in the state of
São Paulo. This state also attracted Syrian and
Lebanese tradesmen and merchants, although some
settled in Rio de Janeiro and in the Amazon region,

where they played a key role in the rubber trade between 1890 and 1910.

Café Latte Republic

The newborn republic established a federal arrangement that has continued to this day. A presidential system was adopted, replacing the old parliamentary one, and the former provinces were made into autonomous states.

This led to a power struggle between the central government and the new, independent states. The result was that the two most powerful states, São Paulo (whose economy was based on coffee) and Minas Gerais (whose wealth came from dairy farming), came to exercise a duopoly on power. They took turns nominating a candidate for the presidency, who was then duly elected. This became known as "coffee-with-milk politics."

The farming oligarchy that effectively controlled the country favored agricultural production and exports, and gave little incentive to the manufacturing sectors. But this "Old Republic" model was thrown into crisis as industry struggled to develop. The early 1920s brought expressions of discontent, with the first industrial strikes inspired by anarchist ideology (largely spread by Italian workers) and by the "lieutenants' movement" (*tenentismo*) inside the military. The lieutenants were mostly from poorer backgrounds and dissatisfied with the way the dominant oligarchy governed the country.

In Search of a Brazilian Identity

Revolutionary fervor and new ideas about national identity found form in a "Week of Modern Art" staged by Brazilian artists themselves in São Paulo in 1922. This was a rejection of the older, conservative, and essentially Europeanized Brazilian culture in favor of a new, fresh, and tropical model. The paintings were in bright, vibrant colors, while the literature featured racially mixed characters. This movement was also heavily influenced by the industrial ideals of progress and development. It did more than revolutionize just the arts. The event can be seen as symbolic of a society turning its back on the past and seeking to redefine itself; the impact of this event went far beyond the intellectual elite.

A poster from the pivotal Week of Modern Art.

The New State

The balance of power between the presidents from São Paulo and Minas Gerais was upset when São Paulo's president failed to name a candidate from Minas to succeed him, appointing a *paulista* instead. Politicians from Minas joined forces with the prominent state of Rio Grande do Sul to name a southerner, former finance minister Getúlio Vargas, as their candidate, who had the support of the *tenentes* (lieutenants). Even though the candidate from São Paulo won the presidential elections in 1930, Vargas took power with the backing of the military. His first act was to dissolve the National Congress and the state and municipal legislatures.

He replaced state governors with appointed officials. Drawing up a new constitution in 1934, he was elected for another term by indirect vote. In 1937, before the end of his new term and in response to civil unrest, he declared a state of emergency, citing a supposed threat of communism. Once again, he shut down the National Congress. But this time he revealed the dictatorial character of his regime by governing by decree, censoring the press, and arresting, torturing, and sending into exile opponents of the New State (Estado Novo), as he called it.

Vargas's policies were conducted in the name of nationalism. All the communication and transportation systems were nationalized. Domestic industry was promoted and the importation of goods restricted. Vargas had a paternalist and populist image that appealed to a sector of the Brazilian people. He was seen as a strong figure who reduced the influence of the traditional oligarchies, partly by introducing secret ballots and women's voting rights. It also helped that his government passed very positive social welfare measures.

In 1945, as a result of military pressure, Vargas agreed to allow presidential elections and not to run himself. General Dutra, former minister of defense, won the elections and introduced more liberal economic policies along with reduced state intervention. In 1950, however, Vargas ran again and won the presidential election. His last term in office was colored by increasing protests about the stagnating economy and by accusations of corruption, so much so that the army, once his staunch supporter, demanded his resignation. Instead he put a bullet through his heart, causing the national commotion that, according to some, he had always sought.

Fifty Years in Five

The year 1955 saw a glimmer of democratic hope in the shape of the newly elected president, Juscelino Kubitschek. Entrepreneurial by nature, he promised to accomplish fifty years of progress in just five. In order to reverse years of economic decline, he encouraged both foreign and domestic investment and the rapid expansion of industry. His government oversaw increases in oil production and the establishment of a national petrochemical industry. Tax incentives for foreign companies helped the development of new industries, including automobile manufacturing.

Kubitschek was called a visionary and a madman, particularly when he announced and presided over the building of a new capital, Brasília. Completed in April

1960, the new capital was built from nothing in four years, in the remote Central West. The promised new era never came about, though. Instead, Brazilians had to cope with high inflation, caused mainly by the debt incurred by the huge road-building program that connected the major cities to each other and to the new capital.

The next president, Jânio Quadros, resigned a few months after winning the election. His vice president, a communist sympathizer, João Goulart, who succeeded him, did not finish his term. A military coup overthrew him in 1964. The darkest years in Brazil's modern history were to follow.

Dictatorship Years

Five generals held office during the period from 1964 to 1985. In the initial years they sought to stabilize the economic situation. In the name of an anticommunist campaign, "institutional acts" (decrees) closed down political parties, outlawed strikes, and allowed the persecution of all opponents of military rule. Student movements were severely repressed and student deaths at the hands of the police and the military provoked a reaction from different civil sectors, including the Catholic Church. More repression led to the beginning of armed resistance, organized mainly by students.

The military shut down the National Congress and issued new institutional acts censoring the media and passing laws that contravened human rights. Political opposition was met with torture and exile. Progressive sectors of the Catholic Church played a fundamental role in opposing the dictatorship. Despite being censored at home, Brazilian Bishop Hélder Câmara was the first to denounce the use of torture publicly to the outside world, during one of his trips to France.

On the financial front, however, inflation was contained and the economy grew at one of the highest rates in the world (there was a 14 percent increase in GDP in 1973), attracting foreign investors. But successive petroleum crises quickly changed the economic landscape, since imported oil was the country's main energy source. The economy spiraled out of control and inflation shot up. As a result, people became increasingly dissatisfied with the government.

Tanks outside the National Congress, Brasília, during the military coup of 1964.

LIBERATION THEOLOGY

The more progressive sectors within the Catholic Church were organized around the ideals of Liberation Theology, which were most widespread in the 1970s and 1980s. This supported a social vision of the Christian promise of salvation and prayed for better economic, social, and political conditions for all people on earth (not just in heaven). Its proponents established ecclesiastical communities (*comunidades eclesiais de base*), which acted as centers of discussion and influenced a whole generation of Catholics, including President Lula da Silva.

A steady reinstatement of civil liberties began in 1974, with the suspension of press censorship. In 1979, there was a general amnesty for political exiles and the military alike. In 1982 the first direct elections for state governors, suspended since 1965, took place.

Despite popular pressure for direct presidential elections, in 1984 the opposition candidate Tancredo Neves was chosen by an electoral college. The first civilian president after twenty-one years of military government did not rule the country; he died weeks after taking office, and was replaced by his vice president. The dictatorship was nevertheless ended, as was the longest transition to democracy in Latin America.

Impeachment or Resignation

The first direct elections for president since 1960 took place in November 1989. Fernando Collor won a narrow victory over the Workers' Party candidate, Lula da Silva. Collor struggled to control the hyperinflation that had overtaken his predecessor's government, but he failed to stabilize the economy and was himself charged with corruption. When the trial for his impeachment started, Collor resigned. The Senate, by a large majority, eventually reached a verdict to impeach him.

Once again, a Brazilian vice president took office. Itamar Franco governed for the remaining two years of the term. His priority was to design an economic plan to control inflation, and this was made the responsibility of finance minister Fernando Henrique Cardoso.

The Real Plan

Fernando Henrique Cardoso, a former social scientist, was elected—and reelected—over Lula da Silva, mainly because of the success of his program to contain inflation. He changed the name of the currency to the Real, and adopted a plan of austerity measures, which became known as the "Real Plan" (Plano Real). The average rate of inflation dropped from 1,280.9 percent per annum (as during the previous five years) to an average of 11.4 percent per annum by the year 2000. His other priorities included the improvement of the national health system and the expansion of elementary education, resulting in a dramatic fall in illiteracy rates.

The Workers' Party

Former metalworker and trade unionist Luiz Inácio Lula da Silva won the presidency in 2002 with over 60 percent of votes. Lula was the first Brazilian from a disadvantaged background to reach the office of president. In a country with a tradition of controlling oligarchies and a military class that intervenes every now and then, electing a poor northeasterner as a president—and having him take office—was a remarkable achievement, regardless of the merits of his government. Those who believed that this was the end of control by a wealthy few over millions of poorer citizens would be deeply disappointed—as would those who expected the end of corruption in Brazilian politics.

One of the most significant steps taken by President Lula was that of ensuring the continuity of economic policy. This broke with the habits of previous governments, which often introduced radical economic shock tactics to solve the country's problems. For the first time in recent history there was no break in economic policy, sending signals to international investors of longer-term stability—and these were definitely picked up by the world markets.

It was, however, the "Bolsa Família" social benefit scheme that was mainly responsible for delivering Lula a second term. Introduced in 2003, Bolsa Família was a guaranteed minimum income scheme aimed at families suffering from extreme and persistent poverty.

Households receiving the benefit had to commit to ensuring that children up to fifteen years old have an 85 percent record of school attendance, while youths aged sixteen to seventeen were required to complete 75 percent of school attendance. Every member of each household also had to attend regular health checks.

Lula's social plans managed to contribute to a significant reduction of poverty in Brazil, reaching around 13 million households, or 25 percent of the total, and thus addressing social exclusion.

Meanwhile, measures to deal with the issue of racial exclusion, which started with the adoption of racial quotas for students entering university during Fernando Henrique's government, were successfully implemented throughout Lula's government and became wider reaching during the term of Lula's successor, President Dilma Rousseff.

Elected in 2011, Dilma Rousseff was the first woman president to take office in Brazil. In her youth, Dilma actively opposed the dictatorship and was jailed and tortured by the regime back then. She rose to power as Minister of Energy and Chief of Staff to President Lula, and in 2013 was ranked second in Forbes' list of the most powerful women in the world after Angela Merkel, then Chancellor of Germany.

Dilma's government attracted the attention of the domestic and international media in 2013 when more than a million people took to the streets of Brazil's cities, initially in protest of an increase in bus fares. Thanks to the power of social media, the protests quickly turned into a nationwide movement against bad public services, inflation, corruption, and other targets, such as outrage at the billions being spent on the World Cup.

Brazil's first woman president, Dilma Roussett.

The estimated 40 million individuals lifted out of poverty by the Bolsa Família policy created a new class of Brazilians with access to education and the consumer market, who were eager to add their voices to the established middle classes in demanding better management of state funds and adequate public services.

There were violent clashes between some protesters and the police, but overall the demonstrations were peaceful.

The scale of the unrest caught Brazilian politicians unprepared. Without a leader with whom to negotiate, they were not equipped to handle the situation, and indeed didn't know what to make of a "social media revolution" demanding transparency in politics and policies that were not apparently linked to parties or ideologies. The protests culminated in a process that led to Dilma's impeachment on the grounds of having violated budgetary law and fiscal responsibility norms. During the impeachment vote, a lesser-known member of the Chamber of Deputies, Jair Bolsonaro, attracted nationwide attention when he dedicated his vote against Rousseff to her military torturer.

Rousseff was removed from office in 2016 and succeeded by her vice president, Michel Temer, from the Brazilian Democratic Movement Party (MDB). Temer himself was subject to impeachment attempts and corruption-related criminal investigations by the Federal Police, but managed to finish his term in office. His government approved reforms that closed some public services like *farmacias populares* ("popular pharmacies"), which sold low-cost medicines to the poorest, and reduced the number of Bolsa Família beneficiaries.

In 2017 Lula was convicted on charges of passive corruption for accepting political bribes in a controversial trial. In 2018 he was arrested and prevented from running in the next presidential election. Sergio Moro, the federal judge of the case, was also the prosecutor and later became Minister of Justice in Jair Bolsonaro's government.

The Rise of the Right

After a masterful low-budget campaign that focused on short videos and memes shared on social media platforms, far-right candidate Jair Bolsonaro attracted considerable support. Despite having served in the Chamber of Deputies since the nineties, Bolsonaro portrayed himself as an outsider on an anti-corruption crusade, who sought to defend traditional family values and oppose same-sex marriage and abortion. His slogan "Brazil above everything, God above everyone" (*"Brasil acima de tudo, Deus acima de todos"*) and the large-scale support of the Evangelical churches captivated the devotion of wide swaths of conservative Brazilians. The retired military captain didn't hide his admiration for the period of military dictatorship and used combative language against those groups he perceived as adversaries, including after taking office in 2019. A savvy politician, he made effective use of social media to energize his voter base and attack his critics.

Brazil's economy improved over the course of Bolsonaro's leadership, but it's likely not what he will be remembered for: he was highly criticized for his response to the Covid-19 pandemic, opposing quarantine measures, and for delaying the purchase of life-saving vaccines. Throughout his term, he greatly encouraged commercial development of the Amazon region and decreased efforts to prosecute illegal logging, farming, and mining, which served to weaken the protection of Indigenous groups. Agrobusiness flourished and in 2021 deforestation hit a fifteen-year high.

In contrast to previous leaders, the right-wing president also adopted strategies that served to distance Brazil from the United Nations. During the pandemic, he threatened to withdraw Brazil from the World Health Organization and from the Paris Climate Agreement, though neither materialized.

Infrastructure issues were tackled and the government supported the improvement of roads, highways, railways, ports, and airports by auctioning dozens of such projects to private firms.

A hotly contested election campaign in 2022 saw Bolsonaro lose to two-time former president Lula, who was permitted to throw his hat into the ring once more after the corruption convictions against him were annulled due to a lack of judicial impartiality. The electoral race served to further polarize society and emotions ran high as each side fought for the reigns. Lula's victory was hard won—he only beat Bolsonaro by 0.9 percent of votes—and what followed illustrates just how deep the country's social fractures really go.

Lula's Comeback

Upon announcement of Lula's victory, Bolsonaro supporters, many of whom didn't believe—or simply refused to accept—the election results, invaded and ransacked government buildings: the National Congress, the Federal Supreme Court, and the presidential palace were all overrun. Allegedly, the pre-planned action relied on the tacit approval of rogue members of the army and the military police who, at the very least, turned a blind eye. The head of the military was replaced as a result, as were around eighty military officials, as the new government took control and turned to the task of pacifying the country.

In an attempt at reconciliation, Lula portrayed his victory as "the victory of an immense democratic movement that was formed above political parties, personal interests, and ideology, so that democracy could be the winner."

The challenges he faced at the start of his third term were significant: a fragile post-pandemic economy and jittery, inflation-ridden global markets, a hostile congress, and a divided country. Observers noted that his years of experience and his skills as a pragmatic negotiator would be critical if he is to overcome these issues.

As for his vision, he confirmed his commitment to social programs and pledged to balance the country's fiscal and social responsibilities, and promised to protect the Amazon and its inhabitants, vowing to achieve zero-deforestation during his term. Time will tell if he will be true to his pledges.

President Luiz Inácio Lula da Silva at his third swearing-in ceremony, 2023.

GOVERNMENT

The present constitution of Brazil was drawn up in 1988 and new government mechanisms were put in place at that time. At the national level, power is administered by the executive, the legislature, and the judiciary. The same system is replicated at state level. As in the USA, the president is elected for a four-year term and appoints ministers of state. He or she may serve only two consecutive terms, being allowed to run for office again after a break of at least one mandate.

Brazil has now thirty-five registered political parties—the high number of competitors means that it's almost impossible for any one party to govern on its own and coalitions are often formed.

Two houses form the National Legislature: the Chamber of Deputies and the Federal Senate. States elect members to the Chamber of Deputies every four years with the number of deputies representing the state in proportion to its population. Three senators are elected from each state to the Senate and serve an eight-year term. In order for there to be continuity, the Senate elections are staggered: every four years one third, then two thirds, of seats are contested. At the moment there are eighty-one senators and 513 deputies, who can run for reelection as many times as they (or their party) want.

The Federal Supreme Court, the highest court in the land, is composed of eleven judges. Below it are the Superior Court of Justice and the regional courts. Special courts deal with specific issues such as labor disputes and electoral or military matters.

In Brazil voting is considered a voluntary right from the ages of sixteen to eighteen and after sixty-four, and a compulsory duty between eighteen and sixty-four. Every citizen between these ages has to vote or give a good reason why they cannot.

THE ECONOMY

According to the World Bank, Brazil was the fourth-largest global recipient of Foreign Direct Investment in 2022. An inflow of over US $90 billion represented an almost doubling of the previous year's figures and was the highest annual level of investment Brazil had seen in over a decade. The main areas of investment are commerce, non-metallic mineral products, chemical products, financial and auxiliary services, motor vehicles and parts, telecommunications, IT services, plus oil and gas extraction. Brazil is the world's top exporter of soy and beef and is a major producer of iron ore, sugar, and coffee. The manufacturing and service sectors also play a big part in the country's economy, which is the largest in Latin America.

Brazil has attempted to become a major player in the world stage, campaigning for a louder voice for developing countries in the United Nations. It was the driving force behind Mercosur—the South American trade bloc. It is part of the G20, which includes the world's twenty largest economies, and has strong relations with China, the United States, and the European Union. Brazil is also a member of "BRICS"—an "alternative" economic bloc that includes Russia, India, China, and South Africa.

Between 2000 and 2012, Brazil experienced an economic boom and was seen as one of the most promising emerging markets with an average GDP growth of over 5 percent a year. The success of Brazil's Bolsa Família social program inspired policy makers in Asia and Africa, and led other Latin American countries to pursue similar poverty reduction schemes. The initiative established a new middle class (and a new marketplace for global commerce) and, along with a growth in Brazilian multinational companies, inspired greater international confidence. "Latin America's economic powerhouse" attracted record levels of foreign investment, as well as more immigrants from surrounding countries.

But then the realities of "*custo Brazil*," the operational costs associated with doing business in Brazil, hit home. Excessive bureaucracy, complicated and inefficient legislation, inefficient public services, high taxes, high interest rates, expensive labor costs, economic cartels, corruption within the public sector, and high transport costs due to poor infrastructure were all challenges for foreign investors and eroded

Brazil's competitiveness. A very public series of corruption scandals and the economic upheavals that followed did not help either.

From 2019 the focus switched to expanding economic power while strengthening Brazil's sovereignty. In practice, this meant focusing on trade and threatening to withdraw from international organizations that were perceived as interfering with domestic policies. While many were unhappy with the direction of Bolsonaro's policies and the tone of his rhetoric, the economy performed relatively well during his term. Agrobusiness boomed and laws protecting the environment were relaxed to allow for development, attracting criticism from the global community.

Looking forward, one of the key challenges the country faces is how to balance the need for economic growth with an environmental policy that contributes to the global struggle against climate change.

CHAPTER TWO

VALUES &
ATTITUDES

THE COUNTRY OF TOMORROW

Brazilians are optimistic and have a basic underlying faith that in time things will turn out for the best. Popular sayings like "Everything works out in the end" (*Tudo dá certo no final*) place hopes for the future in the hands of fate and there is a fundamental belief that the future will provide: "Things will get better tomorrow" (*Amanhã tudo se resolve*).

This attitude permeates many aspects of life in Brazil, including the political. "Brazil is the country of tomorrow," read a political slogan of the nineties. At the time it meant that given Brazil's abundance of arable land and natural resources, it was just a matter of time before it became a key economic power. Then, when Brazil became the sixth-largest economy in the world, some wondered whether tomorrow had finally arrived! Once it became apparent that replicating the standards of developed countries was easier said than done, cynics responded saying that "tomorrow is always tomorrow."

Observers have noted that there are certain downsides that come as part of a trade-off for eternal optimism, one of which being that people can sometimes take an overly passive approach to things when a more active engagement may do more to produce the desired results. Another is that Brazilians are not enthusiastic advocates of long-term planning or projects. The short-termism mentality finds expression in business, political matters, collective memory, and personal life alike. For example, when a new business venture is started, return on capital investment is expected almost immediately.

It can sometimes amaze foreigners how present-time based Brazilians are. They might organize a party for later the same day, or go out but decide where to go only once on the move. Forward planning is not a common feature of social life, except on a few special occasions.

There is one important caveat to make on this subject and that is that visitors shouldn't be misled into thinking that living for the moment means that Brazil is a carefree society. It isn't. Brazilians do worry about the future—the key thing here is that it is not the defining feature of their outlook and competes with and is often superseded by an overarching hope and belief in an optimistic outcome.

FAMILY

Brazilian families are very closely knit. Since state support has traditionally been small and reserved for the very poor, family members have always relied upon one another for help, sharing the good and the bad as they come. It's common for grandparents to help look after their grandchildren, for parents to provide for children no longer living with them, or for sons and daughters to provide their parents a regular income when necessary.

Family comes first and family businesses are common. Some family members will choose to live nearby one another if they can, so grandparents can help look after grandchildren, or for children who have already flown the nest to come by, get fed, and do their laundry at their parents' house. Others are quite happy to move further afield. But whatever the case, family members will always try to come back and spend time together periodically, especially at holidays like Christmas.

Father Figures

While there are women in positions of power both in business and politics, Brazil is still very much a male-dominated society. Most are accustomed to operating under a father figure, be it at work, in politics, or in religion: "*Deus é pai*" (God is father), as they say, and no, it's not a coincidence that paternalistic politicians tend to win elections here. The idea of paternalistic behavior being always negative does not apply in Brazil as it does in many English-speaking and Western countries today, for example. What may be seen as patronizing in the UK or America may well be taken as simple advice or a demonstration of care by a Brazilian.

RELATIONSHIPS

Brazil is a relationship-based society, as opposed to one that is system-oriented. This means that, in personal and business life, considerable time is spent on establishing and maintaining relationships. This is preferably done face-to-face, though today Brazilians are not averse to considerable back-and-forth on WhatsApp, and phone or video calls can be lengthy, too. In business, good personal contacts are also important. Given the choice, Brazilians put people they know first and, if necessary, will bend the rules to accommodate their needs.

Naturally, relationships come with responsibilities and obligations, too. In Brazil, Close friends are expected to be available for one another at all times and can even be expected to help financially when needs must.

In general, it's quite easy to make friends in Brazil as people are usually open to getting to know new people. Becoming a close friend, however, takes time, effort, and a special connection. For more on friendship, see Chapter 4.

JEITINHO BRASILEIRO

The *jeitinho* is the Brazilian means of dealing creatively with life's everyday challenges. Literally translated as "a little way," it can be taken to mean "there has to be another way." In practice, it means that regardless of the rules or systems in place, where there is a will there, somehow, must be a way. There's a tendency to challenge authority in Brazil and when faced with sometimes maddening levels of bureaucracy, it's not difficult to see how this approach came about.

The *jeitinho* is so ingrained in daily life that you can see examples everywhere: managing to get a seat when all the places are already booked up, traveling with more luggage than is allowed, or ordering something not on the restaurant menu. Even in legal matters, if someone wants something that isn't permitted, they will try to figure out a loophole until they can find a way.

The historical lack of social welfare is another reason for the high level of creative individualism in Brazilian society. Everyone has to fend for themselves and do the best they can and if that means having to go over other people's heads or take advantage of certain situations, some will choose to do so. Therefore, even doing things like using a *jeitinho* to pay less tax (inevitably explained by saying that politicians misuse taxpayers' money) becomes what some consider to be an acceptable practice.

SIZE MATTERS

When it comes to defining Brazilians, visitors will quickly realize that there are many regional differences and accents. It's one of the country's many attributes that is related to its sheer size, which cannot be overstated. Throughout the country, there is a feeling of self-sufficiency and until a few decades ago, most Brazilians didn't feel the need to travel abroad. Economic migration, too, was mainly domestic.

Language has played a role in the country's inward focus. After all, it is the only country in Latin America that speaks Portuguese and sometimes it seems to see itself as a continent all of its own. This has in the past caused certain attitudes to prevail in regards to its neigbors, and there's no doubt feelings of rivalry with Argentina, which comes to a head whenever the two's soccer teams meet on the field. But relations between Brazil and the other South American countries have evolved from rivalry to cooperation and partnership in more recent years, thanks in part to special economic arrangements with the member states of the Southern Economic Area (Mercosur).

The size of the country appears to influence other situations as well. Brazilians like to talk about how vast their forests are, how long their rivers, and the fact that you can encounter all types of climate and vegetation when traveling around the country. They also like to "think big," appreciating big plans and big ideas, such as the construction of the Itaipú dam or the city of Brasília, though these are often challenged by people's aversion to long-term planning. Take for example the Trans-Amazonian highway that was to cross the Amazon and better connect the region with the rest of the country. Inaugurated in 1972, difficult conditions and spiraling costs meant that road paving was for a long time abandoned and large sections today remain just a dirt track, making for difficult travel, particularly during the region's wet months (October to May). Fifty years later, the process of paving remaining sections of the track is ongoing.

APPEARANCES ABOVE ALL

There is a Brazilian saying: "The world treats people better when they dress well," (*O mundo trata melhor quem se veste bem*). Brazilians care a good deal about appearances and not simply about what to wear. (It's not a coincidence that Brazil has some of the best plastic surgeons in the world—they get a lot of practice!) It is generally taken that you are what you appear to be and so everyone should do their best to look as attractive, young, and fit as they can. People are encouraged to take care of their appearance as much for vanity's sake as for health reasons and many people take regular exercise in parks, on beaches, and at gyms. Most women and some men dye their hair. This is a country that loves beauty in nature, in architecture, and in people.

One aspect of Brazil's focus on beauty and youth means that, from fashion to TV shows, most things seem to be targeted at the under thirties, and there is a feeling as though it's almost bad manners to become old. In employment terms, this means that it can be harder for a forty-something, and certainly for a fifty-something, to find a new job.

People's focus on the external extends to hygiene, too. While it's true that city streets are not always pristine, and that in *favelas* without basic sanitation you can sometimes smell the poverty, individuals from all walks of life set great store by personal hygiene. Showers are long and frequent, and people will shower and change before going out. Similarly, a shower before bed is considered important. Brazilians also generally brush their teeth before breakfast and after eating any meal. During the coronavirus pandemic, the level of hygiene went up a level still, and a bottle of pocket-sized alcohol gel became something like a must-have fashion accessory.

WHAT'S NEW?

Brazil is still a relatively young country. It is perhaps not surprising then that it maintains an openness and is attracted to new ideas and new ways of doing things. This attitude seems to have started early, during the period of colonization, when the first marriages between Europeans and Indigenous people gave rise to new identities and lifestyles.

It has been said that Brazil was a country where foreigners could change their destiny without losing their identity. Even if their original identity remained, however, something would certainly have been added to it. Newcomers continue to be attracted by the Brazilians' relative tolerance of ethnic mixture and the resulting cultural flexibility, particularly in the big cities. It is an open-mindedness that extends to other areas, such as sexuality or business practices, too. Brazil is thirsty for fresh, original ideas and is so accustomed to these that, maybe, it really can absorb new cultures, or businesses, without being afraid that its own identity will be lost.

PRIDE AND PREJUDICE

For all there is to say about Brazil's love of the new, it is also a place where old habits and ways of thinking die hard. For example, the treatment of different ethnic groups in society is not always very egalitarian, a hangover of the country's colonial days, when skin color and ethnic background often defined a person's individual destiny. Though less explicit, the attitude is still pervasive today. For example, Brazilians with fair skin, light-colored eyes, and surnames that are difficult to pronounce are already halfway there when fighting for a better job. And those who consider themselves "white" will be offended if referred to as mixed race, even if they actually are.

Progress has been made in recent years, and members of Brazil's black community have been successful in promoting black culture, including music, dance, and cuisine. But most dark-skinned Brazilians also come from the poorest sectors of society, so even when they can escape racial prejudice, they still often face additional economic barriers.

By and large, younger Brazilians are more sensitive to the issues of race and discrimination than their elders, and though attitudes are slower to change in rural areas, racism today is frowned upon nationwide, at the surface level, at least.

NOVELAS AND *FAVELAS*

Not too long ago, in Brazilian shantytowns, or *favelas*, you could find people living in total poverty, sometimes with all the members of an extended family sharing only one room. Many of these houses had only very basic conditions, but most still had a TV set.

For many years one of the things that unified Brazilians from all regions and social classes was their passion for TV soap operas, known locally as *novelas*. They aroused a kind of national devotion at a level that was comparable even to the local love of soccer, though it's fair to say that soccer has traditionally been more male-oriented, and *novelas* more female-oriented. Family members of all ages would sit in front of their TVs in the evenings to watch their favorites, which would be broadcast in daily.

Inspired by the American originals, Latin American telenovelas introduced a novel difference to the genre: they end (the story can last from three months to up to a year). Nowadays Brazilian *novelas* have quite a distinct identity and, for outsiders, provide insight into the way people think and live. And while they may appear melodramatic or overemotional, they often also discuss social issues that otherwise wouldn't find a forum for public discussion. Observers have also noted that

Brazilian television, through its *novelas*, has been a fundamental force for national integration, and partially responsible for the urbanization of the national culture, being that they are most often set in the cities, usually Rio.

The Brazilian *novela* structure is traditionally based on three parallel plots, with characters who belong to the upper class, the middle class, and the lower class. The storylines cross over, so that there are relationships between plots and classes, reflecting how social classes within Brazil mix in daily life, as well as providing everyone with characters they can identify with.

Brazilian *novelas* can vary in imagination and scope in a way that soap operas in English-speaking countries rarely do: from historical pieces, adaptations of literature, and melodrama to those that use comedy and political satire, and will even venture into magical realism, science fiction, and fantasy.

Today many Brazilians also enjoy watching foreign soaps, particularly from Portugal, Turkey, and South Korea, which are available on various pay-to-view channels and streaming services.

BETTER LATE THAN NEVER

In general, Brazilians find it hard to organize their time and schedule their day around fixed points.

This could be due to an influence from Indigenous peoples, in whose culture the notion of punctuality does not exist. Whatever the reason, Brazilians struggle to be on time. Being late is part of their culture and whoever deals with them should remember that. The degree of lateness may vary according to the region, but it will always be a feature.

Practically speaking, arriving anything up to ten minutes after the set time is not considered late and an apology isn't expected. For anything more than ten minutes, sending a message ahead will be appreciated. Work meetings in general will begin on time and if you are expecting to meet someone senior, you can expect to wait. The same is true for medical appointments.

BRAZILIAN AND HAPPY ABOUT IT

While it's true that Brazilians are quite fond of complaining about anything from the state of the country, the government, or the weather, people here have a great love for their country and enjoy and are proud of the particularities of their culture.

When it comes to expressing their love, however, things are a little more complex, and people have an interesting relationship with the country's symbols. For example, wearing the colors of the national flag, green and yellow, is often considered bad taste unless it's at Carnaval or a football match. Colloquially, someone is said to be "*bandeiroso*" (flaggy) or "*dando bandeira*" (giving away a flag) when behaving inappropriately or showing off.

Commentators claim that this attitude came about in reaction to the political system during the military dictatorship, which heavily expropriated the country's national symbols. At the time, the use of the flag was actually forbidden unless at a civic occasion. Many things have changed since, and the prohibition on the use of the Brazilian flag has been abolished. For a while, many added flag-printed T-shirts, caps, thongs, and bags to their wardrobes, until more recently, when donning flag-covered clothing became associated with those sympathetic to ultra-nationalist political parties. Some responded saying that the flag was a symbol of the country and anyone should be able to wear it, regardless of their political persuasion. In any event, most Brazilians still avoid wearing the colors green and yellow together.

One thing for visitors to bear in mind on this issue is that, while Brazilians can be highly critical of certain aspects of their country—such as the bureaucracy or social system—criticism is rarely welcome when coming from outsiders. This reflects people's basic pride for their country, which despite the grumbling is high and important to most. As such, it's best to make sure your relationship with a person has developed sufficiently before starting discussions about issues that may be controversial, be they about politics, history, or contemporary society.

SAUDADE

You can't discuss the Brazilian soul without mentioning *saudade*. Although it's normally explained as nostalgia or the sense of missing something, there is no direct translation for this term in English that takes account of its full meaning in the local culture.

Saudade is what you feel when someone you love is away or unattainable, or when an event has slipped into the past. You are sad, and at the same time you feel happy to cherish the memories. *Saudade* can also be felt about a place, too. It is a mix of nostalgia, melancholy, longing, desire, sadness, but happiness too in remembering. *Saudade* is more than an emotional response to a memory, though. It's a feeling that Brazilians actively seek out and thrive on. Music is an excellent medium for the expression of *saudade*, and those unacquainted can explore some of the classics such as the much loved bossa nova hit "Chega de Saudade" by Tom Jobim and Vinícius de Moraes or the northeastern ballad "Ai Que Saudade D'ocê" by Vital Farias.

CHAPTER THREE

CUSTOMS & TRADITIONS

GOD IS EVERYWHERE

"God is Brazilian," a local saying goes. His nationality aside, what is certainly true is that in Brazil, God is everywhere. Brazilians are a deeply religious people and there are many different faiths practiced within the country. Even outside formalized observance there is an affinity with the spiritual and supernatural sides of life and the influences of religion, superstition, and mysticism are so great that they influence nonbelievers, too.

In spite of having the largest Catholic population of any country, the number of Catholics has dropped markedly in recent decades, from 90 percent of the population in 1970 to only 51 percent in 2022. Meanwhile, there has been a significant rise in the Evangelical movement, adherents of which now number around 30 percent of the population. The practice of syncretic religious ceremonies that incorporate African and Indigenous beliefs, though frowned upon by the Church, are popular and widespread.

THE CATHOLIC CHURCH AND THE STATE

Brazil was officially Catholic from the arrival of the Portuguese until the end of the monarchy. During these four centuries, the practice of any other religion was illegal. But colonization was concentrated on the coast, and the institutions of the state and Church were centralized in the capital. So, in practice, due to the very small number of priests, their power and control were limited to those areas. Even so, the Inquisition— the official ecclesiastical tribunal for the suppression of heresy—warned of African influences on the beliefs of Brazilian Catholics.

The African slaves, since they had been forbidden to follow their own religions, disguised their deities by identifying them with Catholic saints and worshiping them in this form. Indigenous peoples, on the other hand, generally welcomed the Catholic saints and worshiped them alongside the spirits of the forest.

Since the founding of the republic, Church and state have remained separate. Although the dominant religion is still Roman Catholicism, many of those

The neo-Romanesque Basilica of the National Shrine of Our Lady Aparecida cathedral, in Aparecida, São Paulo state.

who identify as Catholic don't attend Sunday mass regularly. As well as the recognized world faiths, Brazil is also home to a number of hybrid religions, born out of the merging of Indigenous and African beliefs with Catholicism. The Church does not accept nor recognize these faiths.

The relationship between Church and state has had its ups and downs. Although no longer the official religion, Catholicism continues to have a strong influence on political decisions. It largely supported the state until the time of the dictatorship, when sections of the Church broke away. Even now it lobbies members of the legislature and blocks the promotion of certain policies. Abortion, for example, is still illegal in Brazil.

The liturgical calendar guides the devotion of the country's Catholics and is followed by all other Christian denominations.

AFRICAN AND INDIGENOUS INFLUENCED RELIGIONS

Candomblé

Candomblé started as a unique Brazilian mixture of rites from different African religions. Its rituals and myths stress the ancestral memories of Africa but not the history of African slaves in Brazil.

The religious syncretism of Candomblé meant that each of the originally African divinities (*orixás*) corresponded to a Catholic saint. This structure, along with the party-like style of the ceremonies, attracted black and white followers alike, from the poorer classes to the social elite, and became particularly popular among artists. Today it is possible to find Candomblé adherents even among Brazilian Jews and Japanese. The celebration of the *orixás* has also been exported to the neighboring country of Argentina.

In the ceremonies, the *orixás* manifest themselves through mediums. Not preaching but dancing, they establish a relationship with a cosmic dimension that bridges mythical times and present-day life. The mediums dress ceremonially and observe a strict and solemn ritual with specific gestures marked by

An *orixás* medium at a Candomblé ceremony in Salvador, Bahia.

chanting and drumming. Like any social gathering, it all ends with a meal, when everybody eats the sacred food that has been offered to the *orixás*.

Candomblé seems to be the Afro-Brazilian religion that has kept most of the African traditions intact. Despite using the images of Catholic saints, it has managed to preserve the characteristics of the *orixás* and their elaborate rituals. In some Candomblé houses, the original names and images of the *orixás* have been reinstated (displacing the Catholic ones), attracting the interest of Africans who want to learn about their own religions as it was practiced by their ancestors.

Pajelança

The *pajés*, or shamans, play a fundamental role in *caboclo* culture (see page 17), especially in areas with

A *pajés* conducts a ceremony in a Pataxós village in Porto Seguro.

a strong Indigenous presence. They offer spiritual guidance and act as healers. The use of local plants and the ability to mingle their therapeutic and magic qualities is one of the *pajés'* sacred secrets. They reach a state of connection with the "essence" of the forest and communicate with the spirit world through a mystical trance. The ceremonies include singing, dancing, and miming the qualities of the supernatural forces they want to invoke, normally spirits of animals, natural elements, or long-dead ancestors.

Some *pajés* consider themselves Catholics, and this segment of Pajelança is called Encantaria. The lack of recognition by the Church does not stop Encantaria followers from worshiping Catholic saints, which is also combined with respect for the "enchanted ones," spiritual beings from the forest.

Pajelança rituals vary from region to region and inside and outside the various tribes. In the more urban areas its rites are combined with elements from Afro-Brazilian religions and Spiritualism.

Umbanda

Umbanda originated as a combination of Candomblé and Spiritualism (see page 88). However, Umbanda mythology has its own set of divinities, divided into seven hierarchical "lines," each of them led by a Catholic saint or an *orixá*. As well as having a strict

Facing hundreds of colored wish ribbons in Bahi, an Umbanda adherent says a prayer.

hierarchy, Umbanda features a cast of characters commonly considered marginal to society. The array of entities or "guides" includes *pretos velhos* (old black slaves), *caboclos* from the forest, *exus* (mischievous spirits), *pomba-giras* (streetwise women), and the spirits of children. What binds them together is that they all possess realistic wisdom from every walk of life. In this way they can understand and help with any sort of everyday conflict. The main altar is decorated with images of Christ, Our Lady, Catholic saints, *orixás, caboclos, pretos velhos*, candles, flowers, and sometimes a Brazilian flag (Umbanda followers see theirs as a patriotic religion).

Quimbanda

Also called Macumba, this has a similar belief system to Umbanda, but it explores the ambivalence between good and evil. A very simplistic description could say that Quimbanda "works for evil," while Umbanda is supposed to "work for good." The two cults share the idea of a cosmos separated into two realms that can be accessed through a series of spiritual spells and counter-spells.

KARDECISM (SPIRITUALISM)

Spiritualism in Brazil was inspired by the ideas of nineteenth-century French mystic Allan Kardec

(1804–69), and combines positivism and mysticism via the services of a medium. Kardec's doctrine had such a positive response here that in the twentieth century Brazil became the country where Spiritualism was most widely practiced, particularly among the middle classes. Kardecist spiritualists believe in reincarnation, and set great store on charitable deeds. Mediums guide the spirits of the departed to a more elevated plane of existence.

A lot of the Portuguese-language literature on this religious sect was "psychowritten" by the medium Chico Xavier (1910–2002), who became a best-selling author in Brazil.

PROTESTANTS

It would be a mistake to group all Brazil's different Protestant denominations together under the same banner. They vary in their style of worship and clerical structure as well as in their origins. Protestant missionaries went to Brazil in the nineteenth century, while Lutheran pastors and Anglican vicars arrived along with the German and English communities, followed by Swedish missionaries. Presbyterians, Methodists, Mormons, Baptists, and Seventh Day Adventists have all found fertile territory in which to expand their influence. Indeed, the increase in the number of Evangelical and Pentecostal converts is

Evangelical worshipers in Rio de Janeiro.

a phenomenon of national significance, particularly among the poorer classes.

Brazil's Universal Church of the Kingdom of God, one of the most vocal congregations (it owns a large national TV network, which played a pivotal role in the election of their preferred candidate, former president Jair Bolsonaro), has even expanded overseas, with branches in the USA, the UK, and other European countries. It demands its members be guided only by Jesus Christ and inspired by the Holy Spirit. In Brazilian religious terms, this implies turning their back not only on the idolatrous images of the Catholic saints, but also on the multitude of entities and divinities of mixed origins, and adopting a "consistent" puritanical lifestyle.

THIRD MILLENNIUM RELIGIONS

The followers of these cults combine Ufology with Spiritualism, and believe in the dawn of a new civilization. They support the unification of all religions moved by universal love. Their temples are based around the city of Brasília, "the capital of the third millennium." The main one, Templo da Boa Vontade (Temple of Goodwill) has the shape of a seven-sided pyramid with a massive crystal at its summit and a vast meditation area.

Religion is both fertile and fluid in Brazil. The differences, particularly between Afro-Brazilian cults, are sometimes academic. In practice, the myths tend to blend into one another, giving birth to new cults, even if they keep their original denominations.

Other religions in Brazil include Judaism, Islam, Buddhism, the Japanese "Messianica," and Seicho-no-ie. There is also a growing number of Eastern inspired forms of meditation practice.

SUPERSTITIONS

With such a rich collection of religions and mythologies, it is understandable that Brazilians are superstitious.

Superstitious ritual behavior is part of the daily life of believers and nonbelievers alike and it's not uncommon to find atheists who take the ideas of "bad vibes" and the "evil eye" as real. But there's no reason to fear: knock on wood, and the evil will go away.

FOOTBALL: THE UNIFYING RELIGION

Football (or soccer) can be seen as the "cult" that unifies Brazilians from all belief systems and ethnicities and the passion it inspires in people can certainly be described as religious. In fact, Catholics, Evangelicals, and followers of all different cults pray in the hope that this will help their team to victory, and most football players make the sign of the cross when they run onto the pitch. However, it's the grace and artistry of Brazilian players that really moves their supporters, both at home and abroad.

Football was brought to Brazil by the English and soon became a national passion, played all over the country—including by some Indigenous tribes. It's widely acknowledged that the way Brazilian football is played is quite special; the Brazilian game seems to have been influenced by the movements and dances of African origin, such as samba and capoeira (a dance-like sport created by African slaves to disguise the practice of self-defense). Football attracts many players from disadvantaged backgrounds. In a country with such an unequal distribution of wealth and access to good quality education, football has become one of the few ways to rise up the social ladder.

Brazil is the only country to have won five World Cups, and the fortunes of its national team impact its citizens significantly. When the country wins, everybody is swept up in a general climate of ecstasy and many stores close to take part in the celebrations. The mood is not dissimilar to Carnaval.

When Brazil won the World Cup for the fifth time in 2002, a national holiday was declared. On the

Brazilian football fans celebrate their team during the World Cup.

other hand, when the team loses, people can be seen crying openly and there is a tangible and widespread feeling of sadness.

Such occurrences are not confined to the World Cup. When there is a local derby between two major teams, the streets are empty and people are glued to a TV set anywhere they can find one. The tension is broken only by roars of celebration and the sound of fireworks when a team scores and commentators scream "*gooooaaaaaaal!!!*" for as long as they can.

BRAZILIAN NATIONAL HOLIDAYS	
Date	**Festival**
January 1	New Year
February/March	Carnaval
March/April	Good Friday
May 1	Labor Day
May/June	Corpus Christi
September 7	Independence Day
October 12	Nossa Senhora Aparecida (Our Lady Aparecida, patron saint of Brazil)
November 2	All Souls
November 15	Proclamation of the Republic
December 25	Christmas

OTHER CELEBRATIONS	
April 19	Dia do Índio (Indigenous Peoples' Day)
April 21	Tiradentes
June 12	Dia dos Namorados (Beloved's Day)
June 13, 24, and 29	Festas Juninas (June Parties)
November 20	Dia da Consciência Negra (Black Consciousness Day)

THE FESTIVE CALENDAR

Brazil used to have a lengthy list of national holidays, mainly based around Catholic festivals. Nowadays, after complaints from employers and successive governmental changes, just a few remain. States and municipalities can use their discretion to add holidays to the national calendar, though. They might decide to keep a religious holiday that has been nationally abolished, or they might take a day off to celebrate the foundation of their city or commemorate its patron saint.

Depending on the day, Brazilians will tend to "extend" their holiday. In practice this means that if the holiday falls on a Tuesday, some might take the Monday off, and if it falls on Thursday, many will not work on Friday. This applies particularly to public

institutions, such as schools, and bureaucratic
services. In the big cities, though, one can always find
places like shopping malls that never seem to close
their doors.

New Year—January 1

For a spiritual, optimistic nation, New Year is the time
to prepare for a new beginning and New Year's Eve is
marked by preparations for the evening party. Most
people wear white and sometimes give each other little
tokens to bring luck: something white will bring peace
and something yellow riches. A few will also wear a
piece of colored underwear according to the wish they
make. A midnight feast among family and friends is
the usual way to start the New Year. Others may go to
the beach.

Followers of Afro-Brazilian religions have a
special ritual in which they make offerings, generally
flowers, to the goddess of the sea, Iemanjá. She is
the wife of Oxalá, the god who personifies heaven,
and the mother of all *orixás*. Within the framework
of religious syncretism, Iemanjá is also associated
with Our Lady the Holy Virgin and in the spirit of
all things Brazilian, even some nonbelievers will go
to watch the ceremonies and end up throwing a few
flowers into the sea, just in case. Anyhow, the beach is
the main destination for those who decide to go out
on the last day of the year, if not for the offering of
flowers, then certainly for the firework displays in the

main coastal cities. New Year's Day is also sometimes called *confraternização universal*—a day for universal brotherhood.

Carnaval—February/March

Carnaval, together with football, is the most significant demonstration of popular culture in Brazil. Its importance is so great that Brazilians themselves divide the annual calendar into before and after Carnaval. As a matter of fact, they say that nothing functions and the year does not start until the end of the Carnaval period. If you have to do any work or arrange any meetings at the beginning of the year in Brazil, you may well find this to be true.

Carnaval takes place on the four days before Ash Wednesday and was originally supposed to be the final time of self-indulgence before Lent, the forty-day period of austerity and abstinence leading to Easter. However, the festival seems to have earlier roots in Roman ceremonies to honor the deity Saturn (who was associated with seed corn and sowing), which also involved the worship of Bacchus, the god of wine. During the festivities, the traditional order of Roman society was set aside and slaves and masters shared the same public space. The early Church disapproved of these "*bacchanalias*" and restricted them to the period prior to Lent.

In Brazil the four days of Carnaval are a mixture of partying, dance spectacle, folklore, and art. The whole country stops and people of all ages and social backgrounds share the joy. It is a magical time when social conventions are ignored or turned upside down. The poor can dress up in luxurious costumes and become royalty, and the rich pirates or Indigenous people. Men can turn into women and women can wear as little as they wish. People may steal kisses, flirt, drink, and dance through the night and the following day until it is night once more. It is a nonstop game of make-believe, where anyone can escape into a fantasy world and be whoever and do almost whatever they feel like.

Carnaval takes over the big cities and small towns alike. Every community has its own traditional way of celebrating, but there are two spaces where it usually takes place: on the street and in private clubs. The street is given over to parades and dancing, while in the clubs you will find anything from updated *bacchanalias* to well-behaved, family-oriented balls. The most famous Carnavals take place in Rio de Janeiro, Salvador, and Olinda/Recife. Some Carnaval festivities were canceled during the coronavirus pandemic and have not entirely recovered since.

Rio

The Rio Carnaval is the biggest in the country. It attracts the most tourists and its organization has influenced all other Carnavals based around competing samba schools. Participants work the whole year to make the costumes they wear in the big parade. Various samba schools take part in the parade and are judged by a panel of artists, musicians, and intellectuals. The choice of the winner is based on the creativity and success of the costumes, the enthusiasm of the participants of the subdivisions (*alas*), the movements of the dance, and the music. A fundamental element is the *samba-enredo*: the theme of this song inspires all the costumes and allegories used by the samba school. The parade lasts all through Carnaval and takes place in the Sambódromo, a building specially designed by architect Oscar Niemeyer to help create a dreamlike feeling. Discussions about the samba

Samba schools with colorful floats, dancers, and musicians compete at the annual Carnaval parade in Rio de Janeiro.

school performances hijack the news and take over TV programming. Some have become disillusioned by the hype and feel that the Rio Carnaval has actually turned into a TV show.

Salvador

Despite scholars saying that samba was born in the state of Bahia, the biggest part of the Carnaval in Salvador is not based on it. Here celebrations center around the Trio Elétrico. This started when a couple of musicians, during Carnaval, decided to play the traditionally acoustic rhythm of *frevo* using electric instruments on top of their car. They invited a guest musician along and called themselves the Trio Elétrico. Now, instead of a car, huge trucks with "*axé* music" bands on top parade through the streets of Salvador, attracting a multitude of people who follow them around, dancing. *Axé* music is a mixture of African rhythms with pop music. The most famous Trios Elétricos attract about four thousand followers and parade for hours nonstop.

Recife and Olinda

Recife wakes up early on Saturday to usher in the festivities on the first day of Carnaval. Massive numbers of people go to watch and follow the carnival parade of Galo da Madrugada (Dawn Cockerel).

In neighboring Olinda, giant puppets fill the hills of the city in an amazing street carnival, accompanied

Carnaval groups mark the start of festivities in Recife.

by the sounds of *frevo*. The mornings cater more
to children and older people, with great displays of
improvisation and imagination. *Foliões* (carnival
dancers) make up last-minute outfits and have as much
fun as others who obviously spend a great deal of time
preparing more elaborate costumes. Improvisation
is also a feature of the carnival *blocos* (groups). Some
blocos are traditional and long-established, but new
groups are invented every Carnaval and anyone can
have a go. Apart from *frevo*, people also dance to the
rhythm of *caboclinhos*, music of Indigenous origin.
Possibly the most beautiful moment of this carnival is
A Noite dos Tambores Silenciosos (The Night of the
Silent Drums) on Carnaval Monday in Recife city
center. Different groups of *maracatú*, performing
what was originally a religious dance from the sugar

plantation areas, meet in front of the Nossa Senhora do Rosário dos Pretos Church to reenact a two-hundred-year-old slave ceremony. The drums stop playing at midnight, the lights go off, and everybody observes a minute of silence, after which the players call for the gods in African languages, followed by chanting and drumming.

These are just the most famous Carnaval highlights, but because they are the best known they also draw a large number of visitors, which can compromise part of the spontaneity of the festival.

Good Friday—March/April

This is the only official day off work during Easter, although this varies according to region. In the big cities, Sexta-Feira da Paixão, as it is called, is a day when you can only find fish on all the restaurant menus because of the Catholic restriction on meat on that day. In smaller, more religious communities there may be special masses, processions, musical concerts, and sacred art exhibitions. The most spectacular of all celebrations has to be the dramatization of the Passion of Christ in Brejo da Madre de Deus, near Caruaru, in inland Pernambuco. The small town has only one hotel, plus a few B&Bs, and its size does not prepare any outsider for what they are about to witness.

The Paixão de Cristo takes place in the "theater city" of Nova Jerusalém (New Jerusalem), enclosed by high stone walls, with seven towers and doors. It is said that the actual area of the theater city is one third of that of the Old City in Jerusalem. Inside it, around five hundred actors reenact the Passion of Christ on twelve open stages. The audience join in and become "extras," and follow the actors through sixty scenes from one set to the next, in a "mobile theater" experience. This spectacle used to be performed by local actors for a regional audience. Its fame has grown since professional actors have joined in. It now attracts visitors from different parts of the country, though rarely foreigners.

Dia do Índio (Indigenous Peoples' Day)—April 19

The Dia do Índio is commemorated in every school in the country. It tends to be an opportunity for youngsters and artists to talk about Indigenous culture and for Indigenous people to organize demonstrations.

Tiradentes—April 21

The first conspiracy against the Portuguese government was hatched in 1789, in today's city of Ouro Preto, in Minas Gerais. At the time it was a prosperous gold-mining center, and a few young intellectuals from wealthy families, inspired by the ideas of the American Revolution and French Enlightenment philosophers, got together to discuss the increasing economic exploitation by Portugal.

Left alone, their discussions would probably not have amounted to anything, but the government needed to demonstrate strength and used the conspirators as examples. Tiradentes, the leader, was hanged, becoming the first Brazilian political martyr. The date is remembered as the first demonstration of a separate Brazilian identity.

Labor Day—May 1
This is a national holiday.

Corpus Christi—May/June
This Catholic feast day celebrating the gift of the Holy Eucharist falls on the eighth week after Easter Sunday. It is one of the few remaining ecclesiastical holidays.

Dia dos Namorados (Beloved's Day)—June 12
This is not a national holiday as such but the date is certainly kept across the whole country. A bit like a Brazilian version of Valentine's Day, on the Dia dos Namorados people will give a gift to their girlfriends or boyfriends. Lovers, partners, and married couples are all reminded of the date by shop windows everywhere. Fathers tend to buy their daughters a little gift as well.

Festas Juninas (June Parties)
The June Parties take different forms in each region. They are meant to honor the Catholic Saints Anthony, Paul, John, and Peter.

St. Anthony's Day is celebrated on June 13. Brazilians consider him to be the patron saint of

marriages, helping single women who are looking for
a husband. Unmarried women may light candles and
offer flowers to his image, but if that doesn't result in a
boyfriend some persuasion might be required. In the
interior, where these traditions are still alive, spinsters
"torture" the image of the saint, hanging it upside
down or "drowning" it in a bowl of water. If this
produces a marriage, the saint might even get an altar
to himself. The Dia dos Namorados (St. Valentine's
Day) was established on June 12 because it was the
day before St. Anthony's Day, as part of the same
celebration.

St. Peter's Day is June 29, but in the Northeast most
parties are dedicated to St. John the Baptist on June
24. There, São João is the biggest street party after
Carnaval. Northeasterners decorate their houses and
streets with flags, cook peanut- and sweet-corn-based
foods, and dance the *forró* (an upbeat rhythm from
the interior) all night.

Toward the south, every school has its own June
party. Local churches also organize June parties almost
every weekend. In the Quermesse, they play games,
very much like those at summer fairs, and dance the
quadrilha (square dance) around a bonfire. People
eat food made of sweet potatoes and nuts, especially
peanuts, although more recently there has been the
addition of hot dogs and popcorn. They also drink
mulled wine and *quentão*, an alcoholic drink made
out of ginger, to warm them on the winter evenings.

Independence Day—September 7
Schoolchildren and the military have parades on this day.

Nossa Senhora Aparecida (the Patron Saint of Brazil)—October 12
Literally "Our Lady Who Appeared," Nossa Senhora Aparecida became Brazil's patron saint when, in 1717, a fisherman found a ceramic image of a black Madonna. Soon miracles started to happen in connection with this Madonna and the news about Her powers spread throughout the nation. Her church is situated in Aparecida do Norte, a small town between São Paulo and Rio de Janeiro, and it is visited by more than three million people a year.

All Souls—November 2
All Souls, or Dia de Finados (Day of the Dead), is a festival dedicated to remembering loved ones who have passed away. Many visit cemeteries to take flowers to the tombs of their relatives. In some cities special buses are organized to help people reach the cemeteries.

Dia da Consciência Negra (Black Consciousness Day)—November 20
Black Consciousness Day was originally celebrated on the date of abolition of slavery in Brazil, in May, but its date was later changed to coincide with the death of the runaway slave and resistance leader, Zumbi dos Palmares. It's a day to celebrate the contribution of

black people to Brazil as well as to raise awareness of continued racism faced by the black community.

Proclamation of the Republic —November 15

On this date in 1889, a military coup overthrew the constitutional monarchy and established Brazil as a republic. Nowadays, the date of the proclamation of the republic is chosen to be polling day whenever there are municipal elections. So this civic holiday is often only marked by lining up to vote for your chosen candidates.

Christmas—December 25

Christmas in Brazil is mainly a family celebration, and since the Brazilian concept of family extends beyond parents and their offspring it tends to be a big event, and often with lots of children running around. Although the national holiday is on December 25, the main celebration is on Christmas Eve, with a midnight feast and exchange of gifts. Brazilians don't care for cards but are big on presents, buying them for all their friends and relatives. These will also include the postman, the porter of their building, their house cleaner, and work colleagues. The idea of Christmas gifts for all is so ingrained that all employees receive a "thirteenth salary," an extra month's pay, during the festive season. For people from countries where Christmas falls in winter and is the main annual holiday, the Brazilian version may be a bit of a disappointment in terms of atmosphere and decoration. Despite the heat, Santas in full gear can be found in shops, particularly those with air-conditioning.

LOCAL FESTIVALS

Lavagem do Bonfim—Second Thursday in January
The ritual called "The Washing of Bonfim" takes place only in Salvador, Bahia, but it may very well be the most important ceremony for Candomblé followers. The festival consists of a long procession of about eight hundred thousand people all dressed in white. It ends in front of the Church of Nosso Senhor do Bonfim (Our Lord of Good Endings), where the faithful perform a ritual washing of the steps that lead to the church. (This is another clear indication of the degree of syncretism

Participants at the Washing of Bonfim festival.

and religious tolerance in Brazil.) The church is considered a sacred place in Candomblé—and Our Lord of Bonfim is associated with the divinity Oxalá, father of the *orixás* and creator of humankind. Salvador is the spiritual center of Candomblé and holds several of its festivals, some coinciding with Catholic saints' days.

Parintins Folklore Festival—June

The Parintins Folklore Festival takes place throughout most of June and consists of a series of Indigenous shows and ritual dramatizations. Indigenous music marks every event in a festival that is for the North what Carnaval is for the rest of Brazil.

Parintins, in the state of Amazonas, is a small island in the middle of the Amazon River. To get there people catch a boat in Manaus for a trip that takes at least

Dancers in Parintins take part in the Boi bumbá dance-off.

twenty-four hours, and many spend the nights on board since Parintins does not have accommodation for many visitors.

All the Amazon states share the tradition of Boi bumbá (or Bumba meu boi) presentations during the June festivities. The *bumba* is a popular dance and, although the theme might vary, the basic story recounts the adventures of a slave who kills his boss's ox because his pregnant wife wishes to eat cow's tongue. The slave owner finds out. To escape his anger, the slave tries to bring the ox back to life . . . and he succeeds, at which point everybody present shouts "*Bumba meu boi!*" ("Swing it, my ox!").

The high point of the festival occurs at the end of the month, when two rival *bumba* groups, Garantido and Caprichoso, confront each other, the winner being the one that provokes the best reactions from the audience.

Círio de Nazaré (Candles of Nazareth)—October

This is one of the largest Catholic festivals, attracting around two million people to Belém in the state of Pará for two weeks starting on the second Sunday of October. In 1700 someone found a statue of Our Lady lying by an *igarapé* (waterway) and took it home. To their surprise, the statue disappeared from their house and was found back where they had originally seen it. According to legend, this happened repeatedly, even when the state governor instructed it to be kept under guard. A church was built on the site where the statue was found, and the procession of the statue of Our Lady of Nazareth has been held since 1793. To illuminate the procession during the night, the faithful hold torches and sizable wax candles called *círios*.

Mãe Preta do Castainho (Black Mother of Castainho)—May

This is a party organized by the descendants of the community of Quilombo dos Palmares, the biggest and most successful community of runaway slaves, in the state of Pernambuco. The black slaves' descendants keep their ancestors' cultural traditions, as well as the collective work practices that they created in the past: the families produce sweet corn, beans, cassava, and flour, which is hand milled using their original equipment.

In the Festa da Mãe Preta (Party of the Black Mother), the oldest woman from the Castainho community is chosen to be that year's "Black Mother" and this is celebrated in music and dance.

This is just a small selection from the huge number of festivals that you can find in Brazil. There is also a whole host of cowboy festivals, agricultural festivals, and others that follow different cultural calendars from immigrant communities. These are still observed by their descendants . . . and usually everybody else in the neighborhood, too. Perhaps there is some truth to the cliché that Brazil is a nation that knows how to party. Another way of looking at it could be that Brazilians attach great importance to celebration and are happy to partake in it, regardless of the reason.

CHAPTER FOUR

MAKING FRIENDS

Brazilians in general are very open and welcoming. Strangers can strike up conversations waiting in line, on the beach, and in shops—even a casual conversation in your supermarket can end up with an exchange of phone numbers. Though encouraging for newcomers, these signs can sometimes be misleading, however. Good friendships may very well start like this, but it usually takes far more to be admitted into a person's close circle of friends. With time and effort, though, it can be done.

MEETING PEOPLE

As in any other place, a good way to get to know people who have things in common with you is to join a club, take up a new hobby, enroll in an evening course, or go to the gym.

Unprepared visitors might be surprised when hearing the comment "I'll come too," regarding rather dull activities they may have planned for the day. Going to the post office or the pharmacist may not be a very appealing outing, but if you are enjoying someone's company you can carry on talking as you tag along. People often do things together. If they want to join a gym, for example, they will probably ask their friends if they would also like to. So don't be surprised if your Brazilian colleague comes to the supermarket with you but leaves without buying a thing.

Brazilians don't restrict themselves to their own age group when making friends. Although school buddies might be of a similar age, social groups are often made up of people from different generations as mutual interests and affinities often count more than years. Brazilians also tend to go out in groups, which are usually very inclusive and ever-expanding.

SOCIALIZING WITH WORK COLLEAGUES

There are various situations where you can meet new people and socialize, but the most common is perhaps through the workplace. People who work together enjoy getting to know one another, and sometimes have lunch together. They'll discuss their families, hobbies, favorite movies, and the next step is naturally to arrange something outside work.

Singles socialize more after work than married people and, unsurprisingly, have more flexibility for planning their weekends. If arranging a dinner out with married friends, they may well bring their children along too.

In beach cities there is a culture of occasionally carrying on a work discussion in the bar after work. Refusing such an invitation could give the impression of someone who isn't willing to commit and could well have an impact on how they are treated in the workplace. Maybe it's because the weather outside is more inviting than in the office, or maybe it's a subtle way of reconciling the fact that, although the working day is over, they have not finished everything they were supposed to. In either case, it doesn't count as overtime but par for the course.

The city of São Paulo is generally the odd one out when it comes to meeting new people casually. Perhaps because it's such a big place, *paulistanos* tend to keep to themselves and are less likely to strike up a casual conversation. They may take longer to invite you out from work, but when they do, you are on the way to forming a friendship.

WHEN IN RIO ...

Carnaval and beach images have associated Brazilian women with tiny bikinis and sun-bronzed sensuality. But beach fashion only applies when on the beach, and the same can be said about Carnaval. Sensuality is part of Brazilian culture, but taking the stereotype as the norm would be a major misunderstanding.

Just like everything else, the way the sexes socialize varies in different parts of the country. In the cities people of either sex go out together as regular friends. Further inland, there are places where people won't address a married or engaged woman casually in case a jealous partner takes it personally and reacts violently.

Brazilians make an effort to look good and, while they may expect and be pleased to be complimented, such remarks stay at the level of appreciation only and do not tend to lead anywhere else.

As a general observation, Brazilians are tactile. Men tap each other on the shoulder, and women can touch each other's knees when they are sitting, as a way of emphasizing a point in the conversation. They may also hold arms or hands as a demonstration of friendship. People from both sexes touch arms, shoulders, and hands as they are talking to each other. This is part of Brazilian body language and shouldn't be considered as anything other than that.

INVITATIONS HOME

Particularly in the larger urban centers, friends eat out more than at home, so being invited to someone's house is an invitation to share their private space and to be introduced to their family. You'll be expected to take a small gift and something for the children, if appropriate. A present from your country would be appreciated (traditional handicraft or similar, chocolate for the children), plus a bottle of wine or whiskey. Whatever you choose, avoid the colors purple and black, as some people identify them with mourning.

Strict punctuality is not expected on such occasions: arriving about fifteen minutes after the time arranged would be just right. The evening may start with informal drinks and aperitifs, normally in the living room.

For Brazilians eating is a social activity, but you shouldn't offer to help with the cooking. (The same goes for doing the dishes.) Dinner is usually a relaxed affair and can end quite late.

FOREIGN FASCINATION

In a way, being a foreigner might ease first contacts in Brazil. People here are naturally curious and welcome most things from abroad. Outsiders bring new points of view, or at least they can appreciate Brazilian things from a different perspective.

There are expatriate communities, including those who work in British Council offices or American Consulates, but they will also socialize with Brazilians on a regular basis. These opportunities for cultural exchange are enriching for those who take part. However, someone can live in Brazil for a considerable time, lead a very sociable life, and still have no "close" friends, as being considered a close friend is a substantial step-up.

Reading It Right

Brazilians like to be seen as a nice and friendly people—and they generally are. But sometimes taking them literally can cause confusion. An Englishman who had recently arrived in the country made his first contacts in Brazil and was surprised to be received so openly. Eager to start a social life, he was happy when an acquaintance said he should come to their place sometime. Being English, he tried to arrange a day and time for visiting, but was told only "Turn up at any time." So he did. He couldn't hide his embarrassment when he realized they did not really mean it and he had completely misread their intention, which was similar to the American "Let's do lunch"—a polite way of keeping doors open to a possible relationship in the future. If people really want to arrange something, they will mention a date.

FRIENDSHIP THE BRAZILIAN WAY

As well as the closeness of the family network and the love invested in it, Brazilians set great store by close friendships. To be a friend is both a privilege and a responsibility. Friends have each other's best interests in mind. A friend is someone you celebrate with when something good comes your way. It is also someone you can rely on when bad things happen.

For people from cultures where you are supposed to be all right on your own and where private space is to be respected, Brazilian friendship may seem a little invasive. For a start, there are no off-limit conversations. Moreover, people express their emotions more freely, which means they're also not ashamed to admit when they're not doing OK. Using expressions like "You'll be all right" may sound as though you don't care. Better would be to show that you have confidence in your friend's ability to deal with their problem. True friends are expected to face everything together.

Criticism Can Be Care

An English teacher went to work in the interior of Brazil. On her birthday, to her astonishment, her students told her that she was an attractive woman, but that her clothes and haircut didn't really suit her. So, as a present, they took her shopping and picked out clothes for her. They even took her to a hairdresser and instructed the stylist as to what to do. Despite her apprehension, when she went out the next day with her new makeover, she found that numerous people made comments about how nice she looked, which they had never really done before.

CHAPTER FIVE

DAILY LIFE

WHO'S FAMILY?

For Brazilians family is an all-inclusive notion. "Close family" means parents, children, grandparents, uncles and aunts, cousins—everybody they see regularly for Sunday lunches and at family meetings. Moreover, relationships through marriage may be considered as strong as those through blood. In a case of marital breakup, it's not uncommon for the mother-in-law to take the side of her son- or daughter-in-law instead of her own child's.

Brazilians have the expression *ser parte da família* (to be part of the family), which refers to anyone who is not related by blood or marriage but is considered as such. These may be close friends, godparents, or even a well-loved maid.

The connection between family employers and domestic employees is a complex one. Most middle-class Brazilians hire a part-time cleaner or a maid. While cleaners come on average once a week, maids work five to six days a week and some live with the family. The relationships can vary from downright abusive to becoming a member of the family, but they are rarely just professional. Some children become so attached to their maid (or nanny) that they maintain links with them throughout their adult lives. This is more common in regions where the influence from colonial times is strong, coupled with the fact that poverty is more widespread and the cost of labor is lower.

Portrait of a Brazilian family at a weekend gathering.

MARRIAGE

Weddings are an occasion to rejoice. Regardless of class or age group, a party is always the order of the day. Brazilians will even celebrate when they are not getting married officially: people who decide to live together as partners also stage an event for family and friends, and are given presents to help them in their new life. (They will also refer to themselves as "married" and to each other as "husband" or "wife.") Common law spouses who are in a "stable relationship" (*união estável*) have the same legal rights as those officially married.

In 2011 gay couples gained the right to have their relationships recognized by law the same way as heterosexual couples and, in 2013, the National Council of Justice (Conselho Nacional de Justiça) ruled that gay couples could also get married if they wish to.

Most Brazilians live at home until they get married, regardless of age. Some will live with their parents after marriage, together with their new family. This situation is normally intended as provisional while they work for the means to move on. Sometimes widowed parents or those on low incomes will move in with their children.

MACHO MEN

Machismo is more noticeable toward the North and the interior of the country, where men have the last word, at least in public. In reality power usually rests with the breadwinner. Normally that is the man, though in major cities some women earn more than their partners. In that case, common decisions and responsibilities tend to be shared. Within the household, whatever the income-earning ratio, a few areas remain quite traditional: the woman will decide on the decor and the man will choose the family car.

CHILDREN

The birth of a baby is the ultimate cause for celebration. Babies are mostly born in hospitals. Bigger city hospitals, especially after a caesarian section, try to restrict the number of visitors in the room at one time. Brazilians take turns and try a *jeitinho* to get as many relatives and friends in to see the newborn baby as soon as they can.

Children are the center of family life and a household's daily routine is focused around them. Parents will adapt their mealtimes, particularly when the children are at school, since children tend to eat most meals with their parents. Grandparents play a fundamental role in bringing up the offspring, especially in the lower classes.

The way Brazilians take their children's opinions and preferences into account may surprise people from cultures where "children are seen but not heard." Their opinions will be listened to and have influence. When

A teacher shows schoolchildren how to pot a plant at a school in Rio de Janeiro.

shopping for clothes, children often decide what they like, and when going with their parents to a restaurant, will choose what they want to eat and drink. In fact, Brazilian restaurants are very child friendly. Often, once the child has finished eating, while the adults carry on talking, the child will get up and talk to people from other tables or play with other children. This doesn't upset anyone; on the contrary, it is well received.

Discipline is not the most important issue when it comes to the relationship between Brazilian parents and their children; rather, the relationship is based more on affection and the mutual respect that comes out of it.

In the bigger cities, working parents tend to leave their young children in day care. There are public and private centers, with varying prices. Some of the best include nurses and psychologists on the staff and offer a busy program for entertaining and educating the children. Some workplaces also offer day-care facilities.

Middle- and upper-class schoolchildren can have very full schedules, attending extracurricular activities such as sports, music, dance, and language courses.

Urban families tend to be smaller and the children more spoiled. In rural areas, families can be larger and children are sometimes expected to help with household and work tasks.

A single child is increasingly becoming a choice for the urban middle class, as they struggle to keep up with living expenses.

EDUCATION

Brazilians of all classes attach great importance to education and it's rightly seen as a passport to better employment and a higher standard of living.

Schooling is divided into three sections: fundamental, intermediate, and higher, and the school year runs from February to the beginning of December. Basic education (fundamental) runs from seven to fourteen years old. This can be free, as is intermediate (high school) education. There are also private, fee-paying institutions that are often better resourced and provide better tuition than the state equivalents. University and further education is a mix of state funded and fee-paying, though the best universities in Brazil are free.

Education does not stop once you graduate. Professional Brazilians frequently enroll in courses outside office hours so as to keep up with an ever-changing work environment, stay one step ahead of the new graduate intake, and, hopefully, hold on to their jobs.

Although education is provided at all levels, the percentage of people who continue beyond basic education is low. Illiteracy is still a factor although rates have improved: by 2023 literacy had reached 95 percent. Not surprisingly, illiteracy and school nonattendance rates are higher in poorer and more rural communities. Lack of education bars access to better employment, so

The Federal University of Paraná in Curitiba.

people from these groups often end up in menial jobs, which are so poorly paid that their children have to leave school earlier to start work as well. The government's *bolsa família* initiative (see Chapter 1) took steps to tackle this cycle, but the issue remains.

Military service is compulsory for men at age eighteen. It can vary from six months to one year.

EMPLOYMENT

Contrary to some of the stereotypes believed outside the country, in Brazil most people work very hard. There is no comprehensive social welfare system, which means that once you have a job you work hard to keep it. Often people have more than one job to make ends meet. There is also a sizable black economy made up of people selling things on the street, washing car windows, reading palms, "looking after" parked cars, and so on. They live on the small change they receive and put in many hours just to get by. Those scratching out a living on the streets or on the land are probably not included in official employment statistics.

In the most recent Census, the age range for employment was listed as being from ten to seventy. The official working age is now from 15 to 64, but critics claim that child labor (considered from ages 7 to 14) may be much higher than the official data of 2.5 percent. Education is universally available, but in some poor households children have to work to help support the family, this being more so the case in rural areas than in towns. People also retire earlier in urban areas. Across all ages, the percentage of those in work in 2022 was 57 percent—50 percent male and 43 percent female.

Most of the workforce is divided between three main sectors: the retail and service sector is the largest, followed by industry, and then agricultural. Employment is higher in the South and Southeast and at its lowest in the Northeast. This explains why there has been so much migration from the Northeast to the South in search of work.

The minimum wage (*salário mínimo*) is about US $250 a month. Normally house cleaners and other menial workers will receive this, but in major cities they may well earn more. Salaries vary according to profession and region.

HEALTH SERVICES

Although in theory all Brazilians should have free access to health services, the reality is very different. Everybody who can afford it pays for a private health plan and has regular medical checkups (the philosophy is one of prevention rather than waiting to fall ill and looking for a cure). In private healthcare land, everything works. The patient can see any specialist he wants without going through a general practitioner first. Screenings, tests, and treatments are all available. For those who need to go to a hospital, some patient rooms look like hotel suites. On the other hand, apart from a few model hospitals, the public health system (SUS: Sistema Único de Saúde) has never-ending waiting lists. Nothing seems to function as it should and treatment can leave much to be desired. The middle ground is covered by occupational health plans, provided by employers.

Be aware that whatever the system—public or private—going for a medical appointment can be a day-long trial. Patients are expected to arrive on time, but doctors often arrive late.

HOUSING

Walking down the street, you can see that Brazilians don't like their houses to be just like everyone else's, and certainly not like their neighbor's! Be it self-built or a sophisticated architectural design, "different" is the goal. The result can be an area with colonial-style buildings next to modern ones, next to others copied from distant lands. The city of Blumenau, in Santa Catarina, is built in a mock Bavarian style, because its German settler inhabitants felt like it.

In bigger centers, where space is at a premium and the population more numerous, many people live in apartment buildings. These are far more anonymous and there is little one can do to change the façade of one's home. But the lack of individualism is compensated for by extra security and the sharing of maintenance costs. Some buildings house more people than a small village and have internal gardens and playground areas.

The other element that may attract an outsider's attention is that Brazilians live behind bars. In larger towns, windows and sometimes doors are protected by iron bars to prevent them from being broken into.

O sonho da casa própria (the dream of owning your own home) is something everybody talks about. Housing, however, is expensive, particularly in the big cities, and so many people rent.

Dutch-style houses in the city of Holambra, home to many Dutch immigrants.

Traditional houses in the town of Ouro Preto in Minas Gerais. The town is a UNESCO World Heritage Site.

In the Brazilian rental market the tenant provides all the furniture and fixtures. Even though they are able to decorate the place as they like, most Brazilians long for a place they can call their own. As salaries are generally low and house prices high, for most the dream of owning a home remains just that.

SHOPPING

Just like everywhere else, online shopping is now big business in Brazil, especially since the coronavirus pandemic, when many relied on the Internet to buy what they needed and have it delivered to their door. The most popular online shopping platform locally is Argentina's Mercado Livre, followed by Americanas and Magazine Luiza (known as MagaLu). Shopping giant Amazon is the fourth largest.

Modern housing in the upmarket neighborhood of Barra da Tijuca in Rio de Janeiro.

Despite the growth in digital shopping, Brazilians continue to love the tangible experience of shopping in person. Many towns have a day or two a week, one normally on the weekend, when streets are taken over by open-air *feiras* (similar to farmers' markets) with food stands selling fresh produce. Besides fruits and vegetables, you can also normally buy fish, cheese, and sometimes clothes and small household items. Other places have specially dedicated buildings where the vendors take turns on different days of the week.

For all your other needs there is always the shopping mall, which exists throughout the country. Hypermarket chains are also now common, offering food, clothes, furniture, domestic appliances, and electrical goods.

Small independent shops still exist, although they find it hard to compete with the bigger chains. Bakeries are among the small businesses that continue to have

Shopping at the farmers' market in São José do Egito, Pernambuco.

a captive audience. In São Paulo, for example, it is not uncommon for someone to breakfast in the bakery around the corner before going to work. There, people sit at a counter or at small tables for their typical *paulista* breakfast, which will include café latte (*pingado*), warm bread with butter (*pão na chapa*), cheese bread (*pão de queijo*), and a mixed fruit juice (*vitamina*), and is usually eaten while reading the morning news.

DAILY LIFE AND ROUTINE

Working-class days start early. In big cities, where a cross-town journey can take a long time, some people leave home in the early hours to line up for already crowded buses. Office workers tend to start working between 8:00 and 9:00 a.m., while most shops, particularly inside shopping malls, do not open before 10:00 a.m.

Most start the day with a morning shower. Breakfast varies depending on the region but coffee with milk, bread with butter and/or cheese, and a piece of fruit are national staples.

Many people drive to work, especially the middle classes. City buses are notorious for being few and late. In cities served by underground trains, this is a better way to travel: clean, quick, and always on time. They can, however, be overcrowded during the rush hours. People tend not to eat on public transportation or on the street.

Lunch is usually taken between noon and 3:00 p.m., and can last from fifteen minutes up to two hours. In small towns people tend to return home for lunch. In bigger cities they usually eat out in restaurants. Some companies have their own eating facilities.

Working hours are flexible and some people work late. Dinners can be delayed as a result, but finishing the day somewhere between 7:00 and 8:00 p.m. is normal.

Long working hours mean that families with children also stay up late. Parents like to play with their children when they get home, and quite often everyone goes to bed about the same time.

Single people often spend their evenings attending courses, exercising at the gym, and going out with friends, especially on Fridays.

CHAPTER SIX

TIME OUT

When it comes to socializing and spending time with friends, Brazilians prefer to do so outside the home. Friends will meet at parks, squares, malls, cafés, bars, and restaurants, or perhaps go to a movie together. And, of course, in the coastal towns there is the popular option of hanging out at the beach.

EATING OUT AND EATING IN

As a first option Brazilians from the cities will have a meal with you in a restaurant rather than invite you home. Young professionals eat out most weekdays, and dinner can be late. When eating out, it's common practice to split the bill. If a man and a woman are having a meal, it's traditional for the man to offer to pay, though the offer may well be declined.

Diners at the landmark Confeitaria Colombo in Rio de Janeiro.

There are fast-food outlets, of course, but a good option for those in a hurry at lunch time is the *comida por quilo* (food by the kilo). This is a self-service type of restaurant with a wide array of different dishes where you pay by quantity.

For a quick snack Brazilians may well go to a bar where it's unusual for people to just drink. Instead people will enjoy their drinks with *tira gostos*, or snacks, rather like tapas.

Although there are a rising number of vegetarian and vegan dishes as well as dedicated restaurants, a significant component of Brazilian cooking is meat-based. Nowhere is this more apparent than at a *churrascaria* or *rodízio*, which are barbecue-style restaurants. For a fixed price you help yourself to salads and side dishes from a buffet and then sit and wait. Waiters appear with different types of meat on spits, which they carve in front of you, and keep coming until you can eat no more.

Beans or Pizza?

The most typical Brazilian food is beans and rice, though some people have joked that in fact it should be pizza. There is a popular saying that goes "In the end, everything finishes with pizza." (*No final, tudo acaba em pizza*). It refers to situations that are not properly resolved or where the solution to a problem is rushed and not thought through, just as when you go out with friends without planning anything beforehand and you end up having a pizza.

Buffet-style eating is also a feature of meals at people's homes. When Brazilians entertain at home, it is the custom to prepare many dishes, so that everyone can try a bit of whatever they want. For those with balconies or yards there will always be a barbecue, and hosts and guests take turns in looking after the food. On more formal occasions, the best strategy is to wait for the host to indicate where they want guests to sit.

A QUICK COOK'S TOUR OF BRAZIL

Brazilian cuisine is regionally based and is quite varied. In the Northeast, you may well have *carne de sol*, also called *carne seca* (beef, salted and dried in the sun). In Bahia the food is cooked in palm oil and is often heavily spiced. There are also fish stews (*moqueca de peixe* or *vatapá*). In the South meat is on the menu in the form of large barbecued steaks. Rio lays claim to *feijoada*, the national dish—a black bean stew with different cuts of pork, served with kale and a slice of orange.

For a "quick something," there are always *salgadinhos* (savory pastries), eaten with coffee, fruit juices, soft drinks, or beer in any *lanchonete*

Moqueca stew with shrimp, tomato, onion, garlic, lime, and coriander.

Feijoada black bean stew with cuts of pork.

(snack bar). Brazilians do not snack on candy generally, but you can find *docinhos* (small homemade candies) in all *docerias* (cake and confectionery shops) and some snack bars.

Coxinha: chicken-filled croquettes.

Beijinho and brigadeiro truffles.

DRINKING

When it comes to alcohol, Brazilians prefer beer, especially *estupidamente gelada* (ridiculously frozen). In bars and on beaches, beer bottles come in polystyrene or plastic containers to keep cool.

For something stronger there is *cachaça*—a spirit made from sugar cane. This forms the basis of *caipirinha* (add ice, crushed lime, and sugar). Much in the way that you find connoisseurs of whiskey, you discover lovers of *cachaça*, and there is a great variety of tastes and textures.

Wine is considered a more sophisticated option and while imported wines may have greater status, Brazil is now producing increasingly good wines. Locally produced white and sparkling wines are considered

Refreshing *caipirinha* cocktail made with with *cachaça* and lime.

the best, but red wine production is fast catching up. Whatever the drink, it is usually accompanied with food and is considered part of the overall enjoyment of an evening or occasion.

TIPPING

People normally round prices up, so don't expect small change back. Restaurants and bars usually include a service charge. If not, you should leave a 10 percent tip. You should also tip people who "look after your car" plus hotel and nightclub staff, when appropriate.

WHAT TO WEAR

As discussed in Chapter 2, appearance is important in Brazil. When socializing in cities or when doing business, dressing smart is the norm. In other situations clothes are informal—particularly when the weather is hot—but will still likely be color coordinated. Dressing down can be used to avoid unwanted attention in questionable areas. Very few places ask for formal wear, apart from a few nightclubs. In coastal cities, it's uncommon to go to a restaurant in your beachwear.

WHERE BRAZILIANS MEET UP

The Beach

In coastal towns the beach is the favorite meeting place for people of all ages, a focal point for getting together, flirting, walking, talking, and playing recreational sports. The elderly and families with young children prefer early mornings, while couples prefer late afternoons and evenings for a long walk along the sand. Health campaigns advising on sun care have had an effect, but long-ingrained habits are difficult to break and Brazilians still sunbathe in the hottest hours of the day.

For those who want to escape the sun, there are bars and stands where you can eat *mandioca frita* (fried

People relaxing and socializing at Ipanema Beach in Rio de Janeiro.

cassava), fried fish, and all sorts of seafood. Drinks include cold beer, *caipirinha*, or *água de côco* (coconut water), which comes straight from fresh green coconuts.

Town Squares and Shopping Malls

In the interior, the town square is the place to meet, especially on the weekend. People go there to chat, play games like cards or dominoes, flirt, read the newspaper, or just play on their cellphones. In the cities, air-conditioned shopping malls have taken over from the old town squares as a popular meeting place. People might meet there for lunch before the movies, to have a chat over a light snack, or to go window-shopping.

Sunday in the Park

Enjoyed by all, parks most come alive on Sunday mornings when people arrive with their bicycles, jogging gear, or picnic rugs. The biggest parks have snack bars and restaurants inside them, and sometimes even museums, with workshops open to the public. There are also free concerts from well-known—and lesser-known—musicians on some weekends.

Waterfalls

Brazilians from towns in the interior also try to get out on weekends and often take food, and even a whole barbecue kit, to a waterfall or river. This is usually a day trip and will involve leaving the car and carrying the gear quite a distance. It may look as though you are in the middle of nowhere, but after a good hour walking you may find that someone else has gotten there first and that their barbecue is in full swing.

Markets and Fairs

A favorite weekend or holiday pastime for many people is to go around open markets and craft fairs. This is as much to stop and talk to the vendors about their goods as it is to buy anything.

Vacations

Most Brazilians take their annual vacations in one block of twenty to thirty days, and many will travel for the whole of this period. People with children normally go away during school vacations. The idea of a short break to relax doesn't feature—relaxation comes with time.

SPORTS AND EXERCISE

Physical exercise is considered very important in Brazil. You'll see people walking, jogging, and cycling on beaches or in parks in the early hours of the morning. Gyms are also popular.

Aside from getting fit, sports are also considered an important form of recreation and relaxation. On beaches, space is given over to volleyball and football (and even foot volleyball), and in apartment buildings

Capoeiristas swing, slide, weave, and strike inside a *roda* circle.

there may well be a swimming pool for the residents to share, as well as a space for children to play games. Cycling has become popular and on Sundays special cycle lanes are set up in major cities for the growing band of two-wheel devotees. *Capoeiristas*—practitioners of capoeira, Brazil's unique dancelike martial art that has its roots in West Africa—can be found facing off in parks and city squares alike, often with musical accompaniment.

When it comes to spectator sports there is, of course, football (soccer). Matches are played on Sundays and most major cities have at least one stadium, which teams share. As much as the spectacle of the game itself, there is the extravaganza of the crowd—where sports and music combine, with all manner of drummers and small trumpet bands playing all around the ground during the game.

Formula One motor racing is the second-biggest spectator sport. Brazil is visited once in the season and many enthusiasts will set their watches to catch other grand prix races live on television from around the world.

CULTURAL LIFE

Music

Brazil has an incredibly rich musical heritage. Latin rhythms, particularly the bossa nova, are one of the mainstays of jazz and there is a rich vein of experimental music, not to mention classical and different folk traditions. Brazilians' love for mixture extends to their creative blend of classic regional rhythms with foreign ones to keep forging new sounds like Brazilian funk, which has a lot of listeners among younger Brazilians. *Sertanejo* (country) and *pagode* (a more popular type of samba) can be heard throughout the country, while in the South, *vanerão gaúcho* is commonly heard. In the Northeast, particularly in Bahia, people love to dance to *axé* music, which can be heard country-wide during Carnaval.

Live music is popular and some city councils sponsor live events. Where the artist is well known, the audience does not just watch, they join in, and often you find yourself in the middle of a huge sing-along. With classical composers such as Villa Lobos, Brazil's musical tradition is not confined to popular music or jazz. Even in a region as seemingly remote as the Amazon, opera lovers can delight in a mixture of exoticism and international recognition. The Teatro Amazonas, in Manaus, has an annual opera festival in around April/May.

Theater and Cinema

Most big cities have multiplexes, often in shopping malls, as well as art house cinemas, and they are well attended. The Brazilian film industry has produced many great works of cinema over the years, and directors like Fernando Meirelles (*City of God*, *The*

Rio's neo-Baroque Municipal Theater, located in the city's historical center, Cinelândia.

Constant Gardener, Blindness, The Two Popes) and Walter Salles (*Behind The Sun, The Motorcycle Diaries, On The Road*) are international names. Once thriving, the industry is today not as productive as it once was due to its dependency on government funding, which was drastically reduced in 2019. Theatergoing is popular among the middle and upper classes. In cities, it's not hard to find good local and international productions.

Museums and Galleries

Despite not having the museum culture of Europe or the USA, Brazilian cities have a variety of museums

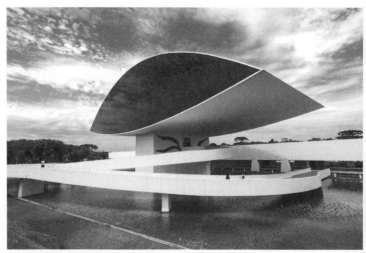

The Oscar Niemeyer Museum in Curitiba.

and art galleries displaying domestic and foreign exhibits. São Paulo in particular is a destination for international touring exhibitions.

Brazil's own baroque sacred art is exceptional, as are its naive, modernist, and contemporary pieces. Brazilian regional popular art is colorful, varied, intriguing, and highly creative.

The Museu do Ipiranga in São Paulo, Museu Imperial in Petrópolis in Rio de Janeiro state, and Museu Histórico Nacional in the city of Rio de Janeiro are essential stops for those interested in Brazilian history. Also in Rio, the extraordinary Museu Nacional has reopened the doors to part of its collection, after a devastating fire in 2018.

Nightlife

In most cities there is plenty to do after dark. Brazilians often go out late, eat out, and take in a show or enjoy some live music. People love to dance and there are clubs for all types of music, from traditional rhythms like samba and *forró*, to rock, hip hop, and funk. In São Paulo and Rio in particular there are thriving club scenes that feature DJs from home and abroad who keep partygoers moving until the early hours to a fusion of house and Latin grooves.

CHAPTER SEVEN

TRAVEL, HEALTH, & SAFETY

GENERAL INFORMATION

Visas and Other Entry Requirements

Visa restrictions change from time to time and you should check the latest requirements before setting out. Brazil has a policy of reciprocity, which means that if a country starts asking for special visas for Brazilians, Brazil will do the same for citizens from that country. Some visitors may need to apply for an e-visa before arrival.

Everyone has to complete an immigration form on arrival, and keep it with them to hand back on departure. Losing it may result in delays leaving the country and a possible fine.

Tourist visas can be extended for up to ninety days. Requests for extensions are made at the Policia Federal. Depending on your location, an appointment may need to be scheduled in advance. Before visiting, a request form must be filled out and the fee paid online at www.gov.br.

Bureaucracy

Brazilian bureaucrats don't like to be hurried and are supremely conscious of their power. It doesn't pay to get frustrated, or demanding. Brazilians have their own *jeitinho* for dealing with this or any other situation that involves lining up and waiting. Often people will go to the front of the line and just ask for some information (*só uma informação*), and the official may well deal with them then and there. Whatever task you need to complete, expect things to take time and keep your cool.

Documents

It's a good idea to carry a form of identification at all times as the police have the right to ask for papers. Rather than carry the original, it's a good idea to have photocopies, which reduces the risk of losing a passport or having original papers stolen.

Insurance

There is only one rule here, particularly with regard to health: be insured. Health services for those who are insured are excellent. Much less positive comments could be made about the treatment available for those who are not.

Cars, however, are often not insured and people don't insure their belongings in the same way that they might

in Europe or the USA. Rental cars normally
come insured, but check what type of insurance it is,
and especially any excess liability in case of accident
or breakdown.

Money

Money can be changed at airports, in hotel lobbies,
and in banks. In a bank, be prepared to line up with
everyone else and to wait a while. Dollars and other
hard currencies are accepted. Brazilians are careful
when it comes to going to the bank, and with reason.
People don't keep their money out on show: they fold
notes and tuck them away, often separating them into
different pockets and wallets. In big cities everyone is
conscious of the possibility of being mugged. They only
ever leave banks, or shops, or anywhere once any cash
is safely put away. There are ATMs in banks, shopping
malls, and on the street, though the latter often look
like mini fortresses. Not all ATMs accept international
credit cards. The banks that do include HSBC, Banco
do Brasil, Bradesco, and Banco 24 Horas, but it's best to
check the sign on the machine. There is usually a limit
on the amount that can be taken out from an ATM
within a 24-hour period, and this amount is reduced
after 10:00 p.m. ATMs inside banks are the safest to use,
and it's a good idea to avoid using street ATMs at night.

Major shops accept international credit cards;
smaller ones may not. It's always good to carry some
cash with you, just in case.

GETTING AROUND

Car

In Brazil, the car is king. Why walk when it's hot and cars have air-conditioning?

Driving is often fast, and it helps to know the way, since not everywhere is clearly signposted. Traffic is chaotic, little respect is paid to lanes, and drivers switch at will and without warning. In major cities traffic jams are frequent and using the horn is routine. Depending on the time, and the day, it can take ages to cross town or to get to the beach. At night people don't always stop at red lights: they slow down and continue moving if nothing is coming. Parking on the street can mean allowing someone to "look after" the car—for a small fee.

People are used to driving long distances: a six-hour drive is not unusual to go somewhere for the weekend. There are still dirt roads in many parts of the interior and the roads that are surfaced often have large potholes in them. There are stories (and photos) of some holes being big enough to swallow a whole car.

The Federal Police can impose on-the-spot fines if a car is not in good working order. Some visitors have reported situations involving having to pay their way out of a problem with the traffic police. This approach should be treated with caution as offering money upfront may be interpreted as a bribe.

The major national rental firms are generally very good, and most international firms also service Brazil (see Insurance, page 154).

Taxi

Taxis are generally cheaper in Brazil than in many other countries—São Paulo being the exception—and a relatively safe way to get around. They are usually marked "Taxi" and have a red number plate. All rides with registered taxis are metered. Ride-hailing service Uber works in most cities, as do 99, Vá de Táxi, and Easy Taxi. These are often cheaper than regular taxis. Uber cabs cannot take taxi lanes, though, which may be something to consider depending on the time of the day. Radio taxis, booked in advance by phone, are also a good option, particularly in the evenings.

In some areas there are also vans and minibuses (*lotação*) that operate a system halfway between taxis and buses, taking people together who are going the same way. Although these are becoming regulated in some cities, many are still illegal and should be avoided.

Bus

In Town

Buses are very cheap but can be quite crowded at rush hour, and difficult for outsiders to use. Different buses have different entrances and procedures for paying, so it's best to have money ready and follow what everyone else does. People on buses are both helpful and mistrustful. If someone is standing with heavy bags, it's quite usual for someone sitting to offer to carry them on their lap. Passengers may sometimes talk, but usually they are unwilling to. It's worth noting that buses are known to drive more erratically than cars.

Long Distance

In Brazil long distances are covered by bus or by plane. Buses are usually taken by those who can't afford the plane, have lots of time, or are afraid of flying (though in a crowded *rodoviária*, intercity bus station, it might look as though everyone travels by bus).

It's always best to book in advance and turn up on time—intercity buses are usually punctual. On these buses people are slightly more willing to have a conversation, though they tend to keep to themselves.

Trains

Although there is no national rail network as such, urban metros and trams are a good way to move around cities like São Paulo, Rio de Janeiro, Brasilia, Belo Horizonte, Porto Alegre, and Recife. However, there are stretches of track that are mainly a tourist attraction. The train that runs from Curitiba to Paranaguá, in Paraná—the Serra Verde Express—is a good example. Built in 1885, the line follows the Serra do Mar mountain range, in the middle of the Atlantic forest, and stops in several places of interest. There are quite a few Maria-Fumaças (steam trains) running in places such as Campinas (São Paulo), Tiradentes (Minas Gerais), and Bento Gonçalves (Rio Grande do Sul). The Madeira–Marmoré train route in Acre (Amazon), built in 1913, is worth a ride.

Plane

As in any large country, planes are used like buses, and increasingly so with the proliferation of budget airlines. Flights are usually efficient and the staff tend to be very friendly. Plane travel is more relaxing and more secure than going by road. People are also much more willing to engage in conversation.

HEALTH AND SAFETY

Mother Nature

Travelers not used to tropical countries may be surprised by the attitude of some Brazilians to the countryside around them. Mother Nature is something to be treated with caution, and Brazilians—especially those from the towns—do just that. Grass can contain poisonous snakes or spiders. People going for a walk in wild areas don't tread softly so as not to disturb the animals: they make lots of noise so that the animals know they are coming and get out of the way. That way both survive. For Brazilians, the idea of spending a few days getting dirty, bitten by insects, and with the possibility of coming face-to-face with some of

God's venemous creations is far from appealing.

Conversely, people who live in areas where there is a high incidence of dengue fever or malaria seem almost blasé about it. Malaria is thought of as something that is treatable and will pass. Dengue is seen as an inconvenience—much like a bad flu. However, visitors, who will not have the same resistance or antibodies, should take all reasonable precautions and seek medical advice before traveling.

After the coronavirus outbreak, people were encouraged to use masks in public places like cinemas, theaters, museums, and on public transport. Some venues may still ask for proof of Covid-19 vaccination, though this is becoming less and less common.

Being Alert and Blending In

Keep your belongings with you at all times and your valuables out of sight. In a country with one of the most unequal distributions of wealth in the world, the desperate resort to any means to make a living.

Most people have stories of either themselves or of someone close to them being mugged or sometimes worse. The media feeds this paranoia by presenting real crime stories in lurid detail.

It's a good idea not to stand out too much as a foreigner. Banks, public transportation (except planes), and even the street are potentially risky places and all Brazilians take precautions. For example, it's not wise to wear flashy jewelry or expensive watches. Some

Brazilians will carry two wallets: if they are mugged, they give away one wallet and still have one left. The general rule is to let belongings go—trying to hang on to them could lead to far worse consequences. It's for this reason too that carrying cash is smart, and preferably in different pockets.

In the street, Brazilians will keep their wits about them. Many women will not walk in the streets by themselves after dark as that could attract attention. They will be aware of who is around them at all times and move to avoid problems if they can. This may sound stressful, but as with anything, it is a question of adapting.

Perhaps it's this pressure that causes Brazilians, who are highly materialistic, to have an ambivalent attitude to possessions. They almost expect their belongings to disappear at some point. There is also the contrast between a people who are on the one hand incredibly friendly, warm, and hospitable, and on the other totally mistrustful of strangers—especially other Brazilians.

If you are mugged, you should go directly to a police station (*delagacia*) to report the crime. Unfortunately, it can be difficult to find a police officer who speaks English. Ask to be put in contact with the Tourist Police (Delegacia de Apoio ao Turismo) to file the report, which you will need for insurance purposes.

It's a good idea to take photos or make copies of all your key documents, such as your passport and credit cards, and leave your valuables in the hotel safe or with someone you trust.

CHAPTER EIGHT

BUSINESS BRIEFING

In Brazil business practices differ by region as well as by the size and structure of different firms. São Paulo is more international and this can be seen in the management style of its companies. However, there are still quite a few family-owned businesses, which adopt an organizational style that is more hierarchical and patriarchal. Rio de Janeiro is at the same time more relaxed and traditional than São Paulo, something that might be explained by the beach culture combined with aristocratic traditions lingering from the time when it was Brazil's capital. As a generalization, the further north you go, the more conservative and hierarchical the business mentality will be.

Most foreigners work for international companies in large metropolitan areas. Regardless of where they are they will follow global management style, slightly colored by local influences.

BUSINESS HOURS

The usual working day consists of eight hours plus one to two hours' break for lunch. In most companies people start work at 9:00 a.m., but some others may start at 8:00 or 10:00 a.m. and work until 6:00 or 7:00 p.m. However, in many firms, although people have a fixed starting time, they often work late. More senior members of staff tend to start working later in the morning and carry on working until later in the evening.

Generally, Brazilian bosses prefer their employees to be at their workplace, but the coronavirus pandemic changed the work routine for many. Even those who continued to work from the office saw online meetings become part of the norm, and this continues to be the case. For the many who have since transitioned to working remotely, at least part of the time, the main complaint is that the time saved from commuting is now spent on long virtual meetings instead, which can be scheduled for "when everybody is available" at sometimes inconvenient times, such as lunch hours or evenings.

The best time for scheduling face-to-face meetings or appointments is between 10:00 a.m. and noon or 3:00 to 5:00 p.m., except in São Paulo, where appointments can usually be arranged throughout the day (and may include business lunches).

STATUS AND HIERARCHY

In contrast to other cultures where self-made business people are particularly admired, in Brazilian society coming from a good family background is also considered important. Moreover, inherited wealth is seen as a considerable plus. Respect comes with status, social class, family, and education. Self-made people try to enhance their status by dressing well, showing intellectual interests, and entertaining stylishly. The formula is valid for foreign visitors, too. Depending on the industry, staying in a first class hotel while on a business trip is a must. Demonstrating an interest in Brazilian history, literature, and music can be useful, but discussing politics can provoke an adverse reaction. Society is currently very polarized in this regard and passions can run high.

The notion of hierarchy is an inherent part of Brazilian business culture. This can be observed when watching people talk, for example, since Brazilians are used to defining social status, age, and rank when addressing each other (see page 186). In a business situation, you shouldn't address people by their first names only until invited to do so. Some people will introduce themselves with the title and name or surname they prefer to be called by. If in doubt, wait to see how others address the person in question. If that's not possible, it is better to be more formal and use the title Senhor(a) or Doutor(a) accompanied by the first name.

Vertical hierarchy is often ingrained into the company structure and management style, with work-related problems expected to be solved by superiors. Important decisions tend to be made by senior members of staff and then implemented by the rest. A team is normally bound together by a strong leader, chosen by seniority and experience. Giving orders is an important part of a team meeting. However, leaders are expected to take care of their subordinates and consider the view of key managers before making a decision.

WOMEN AT WORK

Marcela Santos de Carvalho of CAMEX, the Brazilian Chamber of Foreign Trade.

In the major cities the attitude to women in the workplace is far removed from that of the more conservative interior of Brazil. Whether it's caused by the economic need for women to work outside the home, or by a desire for change in social status, the fact is that Brazilian women have increasingly joined the workforce. Many have college degrees and even outnumber men in areas like education, journalism, law, and medicine. They own small companies, and sometimes inherit their father's family businesses. They do well in politics, too. When it comes to salaries, however, women are still discriminated against. There are also still some who prefer to negotiate with men. On the whole, however, foreign women shouldn't have any problem working in Brazil and can expect the same level of respect that they would receive in other Western countries.

DRESS CODE

Brazilians are fashion conscious and follow European styles. There are several current trends in business attire. Suits are normally tailor-made to have a perfect fit. Women dress "sexy" and elegant on all occasions.

The idea that "you are what you wear" that exists in everyday life applies to business culture with the addition of a new dimension: in Brazil there is a belief that the care someone takes with their appearance also reveals the way they will care about their business.

Foreign male visitors should stick to good-quality dark suits, long-sleeved shirts, conservative ties, polished shoes, and a good leather belt. Women should wear dresses and suits or pantsuits plus impeccable shoes or sandals with medium "city" heels. Avoid blouses with bows and frills or big patterns. Single colors are best.

Special attention should be paid to details. Nails should be clean and manicured. Teeth should be kept immaculate. Women should not overdo their cosmetics. Brazilians wear very light make-up, with a tendency toward a more natural look, but often with a bright colored lipstick.

Depending on the destination and the time of year, light materials and natural fibers are most suited to the hot weather. Good, lightweight wool is preferable in São Paulo and in the South during winter. In the North and Northeast, where it is hot year-round, and depending on the industry, some men wear suit trousers and rolled up long-sleeved shirts. Be aware, though, that the temperature inside offices can be surprisingly chilly because of the air-conditioning. Also, even when Brazilians dress casually at their offices, they will expect visitors to wear proper business attire. Three-piece suits are fashionable in winter but look out of place in summer. Short-sleeved shirts with ties are considered ridiculous.

For business entertaining, dark suits are adequate formal wear. On more informal occasions, smart jeans with a nice shirt and a blazer can be acceptable. For women, a "little black dress" is always perfect.

Brazilian businesspeople wear stylish casual clothes even in their free time. So, a business visitor should make sure to dress well when shopping or

going for a walk and resist the temptation to wear old
sneakers and crumpled jeans.

MAKING CONTACT

The way Brazilians do business is through personal
connections. They like to deal with people they know,
either directly or to whom they have been introduced
by someone they respect. If possible, an introduction
from a mutual acquaintance is just the ticket for
a successful start. It is possible to hire Brazilian
consultants and contacts in specific industries who
can help foreigners find their way through the
paperwork and make the right connections.

Though many still value face-to-face contact,
nowadays the majority accepts—and some even
prefer—that first contact will be done virtually. It
depends on the nature of the business and the size
and individual culture of the company.

In any case, appointments should be made at
least two weeks in advance, and confirmed two days
before. "Dropping in" on business or government
offices without an appointment is not done. Business
trips and appointments should be scheduled away
from holidays and festivals, particularly Carnaval.
Meetings might be lengthy and the traffic between
offices can take a lot of time. It's therefore sensible to
allow two to three hours for each meeting and not

to schedule more than two or three appointments a day. You can also expect them to be canceled or rescheduled at short notice.

MEETINGS

Online meetings follow similar dress code rules as face-to-face ones. (Some women have even reported feeling the need to do their hair and make-up even more carefully for virtual meetings than for those in person!) In addition to dress, the virtual meeting environment should also transmit professionalism: a tidy background is a must.

Particularly in big cities with intense traffic, online meetings can save a lot of time on commuting and prevent the likelihood of either party running late. Yet, given the choice, most Brazilians will opt for meeting in person so they can look their counterpart in the eye, get a better sense about who they are, and make decisions on the spot. Important deals still tend to be finalized in person, where possible.

In some regions people are casual about punctuality. This is generally not the case in Rio and São Paulo, where meetings normally start on time. Either way, when scheduling and arriving for a meeting, it's wise to be prepared for some degree of lateness and not to show that you are annoyed by it if it does happen. Furthermore, while senior executives and managers may arrive late, foreign visitors are expected to arrive on time.

In most offices, a *cafezinho* (literally, "little coffee") will be offered upon arrival. It is usually dark and strong and served in espresso cups. This is a traditional way of showing hospitality. Coffee and water are served several times during the day.

While the British start with small talk and North Americans tend to go straight to the point, Brazilians prefer to do a little socializing beforehand. It tends to happen around the drinking of *cafezinho* (as you arrive and before you leave) and is a mixture of small talk and a little investigation, when the visitor can be casually asked about their background, interests, mutual acquaintances, or anything that will help the Brazilian businessperson get a feel for whom they're dealing with. The amount of social chat varies from region to region and the best practice is just to wait for the Brazilian to indicate they are ready to get down to business.

An exception may be São Paulo, where a "time is money" mentality applies. There, introductory conversation tends to last just a few minutes before business starts in earnest. But don't think that establishing a personal relationship is not important to *paulistas*. The difference is that it will take place during business lunches and entertaining, once they know they are interested in the deal.

The seating plan at meetings is normally hierarchical. In companies used to interacting with foreigners the meeting might be conducted in English. In this case, foreign visitors should remember to speak slower than usual and consider using shorter sentences, making sure they are being fully understood. In some situations, an interpreter may also be present. In this case, remember to direct the conversation and look at the Brazilian businessperson instead of the interpreter. In any case, learning a few words and expressions in Portuguese will help to break the ice and show you are making an effort. For meetings conducted in Portuguese, you will find that Brazilians are fast talkers, so you may need to ask them to slow down a little.

When talking, Brazilians look directly into the eyes of the person they're talking to. Although that may feel intrusive to some visitors, it's important not to shy away, which may give the impression of having something to hide.

It's normal for a meeting to be quite lively, with a few interruptions. Don't be surprised if conversations appear to stray from the topic. Brazilians are comfortable multitasking; one thing prompts another and focus is maintained within a bigger picture. Also, if someone interrupts the meeting to answer the phone, that doesn't mean they're not interested in the business at hand.

During conversations, don't be alarmed at being

interrupted in the middle of a sentence. Brazilians tend to overlap their points of view. In fact, the more interested they are in a subject, the louder and more overlapping the discussion will be. Some of the interjections may also sound confrontational depending on where you come from, but, again, it's only their way of reacting (and paying attention) to the conversation. Brazilians tend to avoid direct confrontation and prefer a more indirect way of demonstrating disagreement.

Brazilians like to analyze situations thoroughly and don't rush meetings until they are ready to be concluded, regardless of time schedules.

Exchanging business cards—printed in both English and Portuguese—is still part of the protocol when being introduced or on leaving. Outsiders should resist the temptation to rush away once the meeting is over. Taking your time to greet and say goodbye is part of the effort of building a relationship and typical of Brazilian business culture.

PRESENTATION STYLE

Brazilians tend to consider the personality and attitudes of their counterparts in order to decide if they want to deal with them in business. Charts, favorable data, and good organizational skills are fundamental, but alone they won't be enough.

Brazilians are happy to talk and hear about personal achievements and show their human side. Confidence, eloquence, and an ability to explain oneself are important, too.

Presentations should be expressive. More attention is paid to content, but style counts a great deal. They should also be kept short (around thirty minutes), use visual materials, and be followed by discussion and debate. Brazilians are interested in new ideas provided that they are supported by facts and research. They can talk at length—and at high volume—using expressive body language. In return, they expect people to explain themselves fully.

During presentations, persuasion, politeness, respect, courtesy, and boldness are qualities that Brazilian businesspeople look for.

NEGOTIATIONS

Changing a negotiating team can ruin a perfectly good deal in Brazil, since the trust is placed as much in the negotiators as in the company they represent. Also, it's considered bad business practice to do so.

When doing business in Brazil, be aware that it may take a few trips to negotiate an agreement. Brazilians are quite analytical and tend to look at each situation individually. They prefer to let negotiations develop at a relatively slow pace, leaving details to be

Work and Play

When I arrived at work one morning, in an NGO in Olinda, Pernambuco, I was informed that the annual report needed to renew financial support from a multinational company was due on the following day. The writing hadn't really begun, so everybody was asked to spend the day in a meeting to produce the document.

Halfway through the day we heard animated sounds coming from outside. One by one my colleagues went to the window, noticed a *troça* (small group of people playing and rehearsing for Carnaval) going down the hill and left the meeting to follow the dance! In a minute I was the only one left. Uncertain of what to do, and panicking a little, I continued working.

They all returned half an hour later, full of energy. They worked frantically through the night, produced a first-class report, and the multinational renewed its support.

considered later in the game. Some hype is expected at the beginning, in the knowledge that not all the initial information will be totally accurate. They will argue their case passionately and enjoy the debate, always looking for constructive solutions rather than confrontation or an outright "no."

Brazilians prefer to solve their disagreements through conversation, without putting things in writing and very rarely going to a third party. Agreements and concessions will be made slowly, through successive meetings. Even when decisions are reached quickly, they may be modified in detail before being implemented. It is crucial, therefore, not to impose tight deadlines when negotiating.

CONTRACTS

When doing business in Brazil, foreigners should find local accountants and lawyers to work with on contractual issues. Using nonlocal professionals may be interpreted as mistrust and cause offense. Also, if there seems to be a problem that is impossible to solve, Brazilian accountants and lawyers will usually find a way around it (*jeitinho*).

It's part of the Brazilian protocol that documents are not normally signed immediately after the parties reach an agreement, but are prepared to be signed later. A written agreement, however, may still not be binding. It may change from the version that was agreed upon, and may change again subsequently. In Brazil, in contrast to cultures that view the contract as the last word, a contract can be revisited and modified as work progresses, and deadlines can change.

GIFTS

During the initial meetings it's not necessary to bring a gift. It's better to offer to buy lunch—or even dinner—while trying to find out their taste. A social occasion may be the best opportunity for gift giving. It's important, though, not to choose anything that is apparently expensive and can be mistaken for a bribe, or which may cause embarrassment.

Coffee table books, nice pens, stationery and other promotional freebies, or alcohol, are good choices.

Avoid practical or personal presents (such as perfume or sunglasses) and anything in the colors black and purple (associated with mourning).

If invited to a Brazilian's home, consider it a rare and special honor and indication of friendship. Bring some wine, champagne, whiskey, or chocolate, together with a small house present plus something for the children (see Chapter 4, Invitations Home, for more). Send flowers with a thank-you card on the following day.

BUSINESS ENTERTAINING

In Brazil, time spent socializing goes toward constructing successful business relationships. People say things like "for friends, everything; for enemies, the law," which goes some way to showing that, in business, Brazilians value relationships over formal agreements.

Restaurant entertainment, rather than at home, is the norm. Breakfast meetings are rare. Lunch and dinner meetings are part of the routine. Punctuality is expected at business meals or meetings at restaurants. Shaking hands with everyone present on arrival and when leaving is the traditional greeting, but after Covid-19 it is no longer the absolute norm. If in doubt, observe what your counterparts do before following suit.

Meals can be quite lengthy: at least two hours for lunch and about three for dinner. Lunch is normally scheduled between noon and 2:00 p.m. Dinner can start any time after 7:00 p.m., while dinner parties can take place around 10:00 p.m. and often go on into the early hours.

A business meal is an opportunity for both parties to get acquainted and comfortable with each other. It's all about developing the relationship. Brazilians may ask questions that sound too personal or intrusive. You don't always need to answer, you can politely avoid the question, or give an evasive answer.

Business itself is not usually discussed during meals. Visitors should wait for their Brazilian companions to raise business issues, which tends to happen during coffee toward the end of the meal.

Brazilians always wash their hands before eating and rarely touch food with their fingers, using paper napkins to get hold of any bread or *salgadinhos* (savory pastries) that may be served as a starter. They use their knife, not their fork, to cut everything, including fruit. A napkin is used in between eating and drinking; using a toothpick in public is considered bad manners (but acceptable when covering your mouth with your other hand). If toasted by your companions, you should always return the compliment with another toast.

If entertaining a business associate, choose a prestigious restaurant, if possible with a cuisine typical of your country. If in doubt, ask their secretary to recommend a place. When hosting a meal, make sure that the most important seat is reserved for the highest-ranking guest. Waiters do not usually bring checks until they are asked for and tipping is normally 10 percent.

If you decide to invite Brazilians to dinner or a party at home, do not ask them to bring food or drink, or expect them to be on time. And never suggest a time for the party to finish.

KEEPING IN TOUCH

Foreign businesspeople shouldn't expect to do much business on a first visit, but should allocate enough time and money to establish a long-term business relationship. Coming back regularly is part of the package, since many Brazilian executives dislike sporadic short visits by foreign sales representatives.

Brazilians build relationships mainly through personal contact, either in person or via video calls. Phone calls are the second-best option for keeping in touch. "Cold" letters and e-mails may not get an answer.

When phoning a Brazilian contact, it's important to spend a little time on social conversation before launching into business, and not to cut the call short once the subject is sorted out.

USEFUL TIPS

- The office secretary is the person to consult regarding any questions you may have. Treat them well and they will help you through.
- Slow pace and informality are characteristics of Brazilian business culture (with the exception of São Paulo), but there may be a formal atmosphere during the first meetings.
- When lost for a topic of conversation, traveling, food, arts, and sports (Brazilians say football, not soccer) can be useful. Avoid talking about personal matters, ethnicity, the economy, and local politics.
- Brazilians are not Hispanics and don't like being addressed in Spanish. Nor should you use the word Latins to refer to them.
- Brazilians are Americans (from South America) and have an aversion to the term America being used to designate the USA.
- Note, when looking at figures, that in Brazil periods (full stops) are used to designate thousands and commas to indicate fractions.

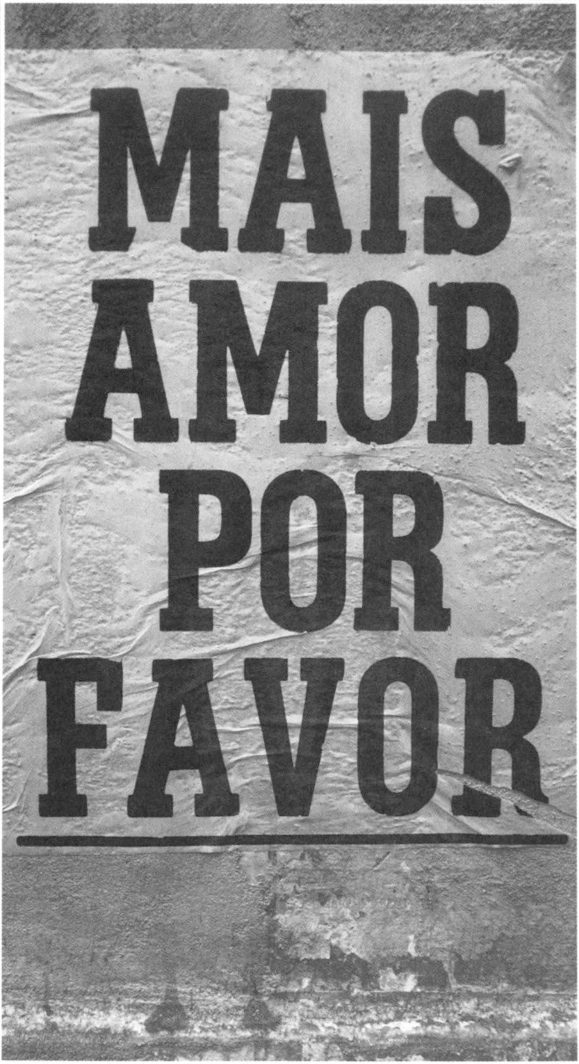
MAIS
AMOR
POR
FAVOR

CHAPTER NINE

COMMUNICATING

LANGUAGE

In Brazil, people speak Portuguese and generally not a lot else. In tourist offices and in the main cities you will find some who speak a bit of English, but generally few people do and certainly not in restaurants, shops, or other places where a visitor might interact with locals. Neither do Brazilians tend to speak Spanish. Learning to speak Portuguese is useful, even if only a few words and phrases, and will help improve your experience—locals who see that you are making an effort will be more likely to reciprocate!

BODY LANGUAGE

Brazilians have a relaxed body language. They are a tactile people and putting a hand on someone when talking to them is usually an indication of interest in the conversation, nothing more. A handshake between men may well be accompanied by the other hand being placed on the shoulder.

In terms of personal space, people can stand in close proximity to each other and not feel that their private space is being invaded. On the contrary, backing away can be considered rude. Things changed a bit at the beginning of the pandemic, when social distancing was encouraged. Brazilians soon went back to behaving as they did before, but with a face mask on (for a time, at least). Though some may prefer to keep a slight distance with those they don't know, in general, people today remain as tactile as ever.

Brazilians maintain eye contact when listening or talking to someone, and accompany their conversation with a whole series of gestures. Across cultures, the same gesture may have different meanings and the one to avoid in Brazil is the thumb-to-index-finger ring sign that means "good" in Anglo societies. In Brazil it has a rather rude meaning that can get you into trouble. It's also considered bad manners to yawn or stretch in public.

HELLOS AND GOODBYES

Introductions can be quite formal. Men will normally shake hands, though since the pandemic, some may just nod their heads and smile. Women will generally kiss on the cheek twice or even three times, depending on age, place, and social group, though just once in São Paulo. (Post pandemic, some also now prefer to smile and nod.) Men will either shake hands with or kiss women on the cheek when greeting for the first time. In groups, people will often introduce themselves to each member in this way. The same ritual is repeated when leaving and is accompanied by quite long statements about how much the meeting was enjoyed, how it was good to see you, and how you should take care, as well as passing on best wishes to family (or friends and partners) who were unable to be there. In the middle of good-byes, someone can remember to say something and restart a conversation. In this case, once the topic is finished, the farewell proceedings will start again from the beginning. This good-bye ritual is often maintained in phone conversations as well. Even among close friends, the host tends to accompany the guest to the door. Announcing you are leaving and simply walking to the door without waiting for your host to accompany you can be considered rude.

CONVERSATION STYLES

Conversation, especially in groups, is lively, dynamic, and often noisy. Normally everybody seems to be talking at once. Interruption is frequent—often people don't get to finish what they're saying before someone else jumps in. However, no one is offended by this. Conversations may become wide-ranging and stray across many different points before returning to the original one.

Brazilians have a flirty way of talking, which particularly applies to communication between genders. They quite comfortably compliment each other about their looks, hairstyle, or choice of clothes. Sometimes they even imply something more sexual, or suggest going out together, without really meaning it. What can make things a little tricky for newcomers is that the only difference between a real flirtatious conversation and a pretend one will be the latter's slightly more jokey tone of voice.

FORMS OF ADDRESS

Even though the approach to many matters in Brazil may be very informal, it is still a class-based culture and places importance on anything denoting power, social class, or material wealth. As such, there are a few things to bear in mind when it comes to addressing people. For example, older people are addressed by the title Seu (Mr.), Dona (Ms.), or even Doutor/a (Dr.)—even for people who have no academic title and are not in the medical profession—

before their first names (for example, Seu Daniel, Dona Alice, Doutora Ana). When using any type of formal address, Brazilians have a deferential form of "you" that is used in the third person (*o senhor/a senhora* followed by the verb in the third person), similar to a waiter asking in English "What does sir require?"

HUMOR

Brazilians have a vivid and often quite black sense of humor, which isn't always politically correct. They are happy to make jokes about most things, including themselves, and there is a thriving wave of satire aimed at whichever politician is in power. Making fun of religion, though, is better avoided.

In rural areas, there is often a simpler sense of humor: the differences can be seen in TV comedies, which vary enormously from slapstick to more sophisticated lampooning of political leaders and social institutions.

MEDIA

The media landscape is Brazil has changed markedly in recent years. Most Brazilian households still have a TV set, but they are increasingly using them to watch streaming channels like Netflix or YouTube. Meanwhile, many now also get their news on WhatsApp and Telegram (see page 192 for more).

On television there are fourteen free-to-air networks, the most popular of which is TV Globo—one of the largest television networks in the world—followed by TV Record and SBT. With some 14 million subscribers in 2022, Brazil's pay TV market is second in size only to Mexico of South and Central American countries. It has shrunk over the previous decade due to the rise of streaming services, though the net revenue of the industry still outperformed both mobile and Internet combined in 2022. Sports and news channels dominate the sector. Group Globo runs the Pay TV channel GloboNews as well as streaming service Globoplay (a local rival to Netflix) that now streams *novela* classics. Prime Video (Amazon) also offers several old telenovelas from various countries.

As Brazil is so large, newspapers are generally regional, though some have a national reputation and a wider circulation. The most prominent print newspapers are *O Estado de São Paulo* (center-right leaning), *Folha de São Paulo* and *O Globo* (left leaning), the popular tabloid *Super Notícia,* and financial and business paper *Valor Econômico.* Many readers today subscribe to their papers online or access the news via portals such as Globo News Online, UOL Notícias, and Record News Online.

Popular Magazines include *Veja*, *Época*, *Exame*, *Piauí*, and *Istoé*.

For online news in English, see Folha International and The Brazil Report. There is also an online site for English-language cultural magazine Brazzil (brazzil.com).

In 2023 approximately 70 percent of Brazilians had some form of social media account, the most popular of which were Instagram, Facebook, and TikTok. According to DataReportal, 54 percent of users said their primary reason for using social media was to read news stories, while 65 percent of users expressed concern about differentiating between what was real and was fake.

MAIL

In today's digital world, the idea of writing and sending a letter seems a very novel thing indeed. That might be why it's experiencing a bit of a revival among some young Brazilians who'll handwrite and send a letter to mark a special occasion. For the most part, however, the postal service (Correios) is used for sending parcels and official documents.

Many Brazilians don't trust the regular mail service of the Correios. Important letters or parcels should be sent via registered mail, which costs more but is reliable. The Correios website (correios.com.br) is very well organized, if you can read Portuguese, and if you can't, Google will translate it for you. Numerous couriers also operate in Brazil, one very popular one being SEDEX, which offers same and next day deliveries throughout the country.

PHONE AND SIM CARDS

In order to avoid paying high roaming fees, it's a good idea to buy a local prepaid SIM card on arrival. There are cellphone and network stores that sell SIM cards in most airports and shopping malls. The networks Claro and Tim are both good options. You'll need to have your passport in order to register your SIM card at the time of purchase, or the line will stop working within a week. Alternatively, visitors can buy an international eSIM card before arrival. Wi-Fi can be found in most city cafés and hotels.

Once you have a SIM set up, making intercity calls or phoning someone in another state is a three-step process. First dial zero and the operator code of the network provider. Then, the area code of the city, and finally, the number of the person you want to call.

For international calls, you need to dial the international access code (00), then the operator code, the country code, the area code (minus the initial 0), and the phone number.

For plugging in your phone or laptop, you will

Brazilians spent an average 5.5 hours a day on their smartphones in 2023.

need an AC adapter and a plug adapter. Some areas of Brazil are on 110 volts, while others are 220 volts, so you should check before you plug in. Also, electricity is not always constant in Brazil, and to cope with peaks and falls in current, most Brazilians have a voltage stabilizer connected between the electricity mains and their computer.

USEFUL TELEPHONE NUMBERS
Police 190
Federal Highway Patrol 191
Ambulance 192
Fire Brigade 193
International call via operator 0800 70 32 111
National call via operator 0800 70 32 110
National and international collect calls 0800 703 21 21
Rio de Janeiro and São Paulo also have a special dedicated Tourist Police line:
Rio de Janeiro (021) 3399 7170 (24 hours)
São Paulo (011) 3214 0209 (011) 3107 5642

"ZAP ME!"

Like most people around the world today, Brazilians have a very close relationship with their cellphones. When it comes to communicating, WhatsApp is the most popular messaging app and is used by virtually all smartphone users. Telegram follows in popularity and is used by around 60 percent of users. Brazilians generally prefer to call than to send written text messages, and today many prefer to send audio messages. Recording and listening to sometimes very lengthy recorded messages—most often without headphones—has become quite normal; it's not unusual to hear other people's entire conversations when out and about today.

In a country where a large part of society works in the informal sector, WhatsApp is also commonly used for work. WhatsApp Business—a sister app that allows small- and medium-sized businesses to share their catalogs, interact with their clients directly, and make and receive payments—was fast embraced in Brazil.

WhatsApp's influence extends into the realm of politics, too. Used heavily by activists to spread both news and "fake news," during the 2018 elections the Meta-owned company was accused of allowing bots to disseminate misinformation freely. The incident prompted WhatsApp to introduce measures such as limiting the size of group chats and how many times a message could be forwarded. Use of the Telegram app was temporarily suspended during the 2022 elections after the company failed to comply with requests by the Brazilian Supreme Court to do more to counter the spread of misinformation and fabricated news that was rampant on the platform at the time.

CONCLUSION

Once seen as under-developed, Brazil has come a long way in recent decades. In the early noughties, during the country's economic boom, many Brazilians thought the path forward was inevitable and straight-forward. They have since discovered this not to be the case, and it has been a bumpy ride.

Along with material growth has been the constant evolving of the country's cultural makeup. Holding a mirror up to the country, contradictions are apparent. Regional differences, issues of race and gender inequality, and antagonistic ideologies form part of the country's daily reality, as does the great warmth of its people, a vibrant and rich cultural life, and an outlook that looks for the good in life and ways to get ahead.

If it sounds confusing, don't worry. This is a country to experience bit by bit, contradiction by contradiction, and hopefully to begin to blend into and become a part of.

Having reached the end of this book, you will, we hope, have found a starting point from which to explore the different Brazils. This will not be hard, since Brazilians are so welcoming. But because they are so welcoming and easy to befriend, leaving can be unsettling. On the other hand, what better opportunity to finally understand the meaning of the word *saudade*?

FURTHER READING

Bellos, Alex and Socrates. *Futebol, A Brazilian Way of Life*. Bloomsbury, 2014.

Creelman, Andrew. *Trying to Understand Brazilian Culture: Memoir of a Brit in Sao Paulo*. Independent, 2019.

Davidson, James Dale. *Brazil is the New America*. New Jersey: Wiley & Sons, 2012.

French, John D. *Lula and His Politics of Cunning*. University of North Carolina Press, 2020.

Lapper, Richard. *Beef, Bible and Bullets: Brazil in the Age of Bolsonaro*. Manchester University Press, 2021.

Palin, Michael. *Brazil*. London: Weidenfeld & Nicolson, 2013.

Pereira, Anthony W. *Modern Brazil: A Very Short Introduction*. Oxford: Oxford University Press, 2020.

Reid, Michael. *Brazil: The Troubled Rise of a Global Power*. Yale University Press, 2015.

Ribeiro, Darcy. *The Brazilian People: The Formation and Meaning of Brazil*. Gainesville, Florida: University of Florida, Center for Latin American Studies, 2000.

Rottgen, Raphael. *The Brazilian Dream: How I left my Finance Job in London and became an Entrepreneur in Brazil*. Charleston: Createspace, 2012.

Skidmore, Thomas E. *Brazil, Five Centuries of Change*. New York/Oxford: Oxford University Press, 2009.

Smith, Amy Erica. *Religion and Brazilian Democracy; Mobilizing the People of God*. Cambridge: Cambridge University Press, 2022.

Starline, Heloisa and Lilia Moritz Schwartz. *Brazil: A Biography*. London: Picador, 2020.

USEFUL APPS

Communication and Socializing

WhatsApp is Brazil's most popular messaging app, followed by **Telegram**.

Get help translating words, menus, and signs with **Google Translate**. Pick up new words and phrases with **Duolingo** or **Ginger**.

Looking for love? **Tinder**, **Badoo**, and **Par Perfeito** are the most popular dating apps.

Travel and Transportation

Hail a cab with **Uber**, **99**, **Vá de Táxi**, or **Easy Taxi**.

Plan your journey and view timetables with **Moovit**. Bus timetables in São Paulo can be viewed on **Cadê o Ônibus**.

If you're driving, navigate using **Waze** and find a place to park with **OndeParar**.

Buy tickets for long distance bus journeys with **Clickbus**.

Find and book accommodation with **Booking**, **Airbnb**, **Trivago**, and **Guia de Motéis**.

Food, Shopping, and Entertainment

Have meals delivered with **HelloFood** and find restaurants with **Kekanto**.

Explore activities, restaurants, bars, shopping, and transportation for numerous cities with **Apontador**.

Veja Comer & Beber, created by popular magazine *Veja*, provides restaurant and bar reviews for São Paolo and Rio.

Book cinema, theater, and concert tickets all over Brazil with **Ingresso**.

PICTURE CREDITS

INDEX

Acknowledgments

With special thanks to Robert Williams, João Araújo dos Santos, and Fernando Branco, as well as Miguel Barbosa and Claudio Margolis (in memoriam).